The Strongest Tree

– JENNY ROSE –

FASTPRINT PUBLISHING
PETERBOROUGH, ENGLAND

www.fast-print.net/store.php

THE STRONGEST TREE
Copyright © Jenny Rose 2010

ISBN 978-184426-935-8

First published 2010 by
FASTPRINT PUBLISHING
Peterborough, England.

An environmentally friendly book printed and bound in England by
www.printondemand-worldwide.com

This book is made entirely of chain-of-custody materials

'The Strongest Tree'
Jenny Rose

This book is written in praise of Jesus Christ.

Acknowledgements

My grateful thanks to Sarah, Jen, Mary, Andrew, Liz, Tim & Emma, Carol, Peter & Paula, Constance, Judith, Tony, Fiona, Jean and …….. Steve.

I also express my gratitude for permission to use the quotations from various sources throughout this book. The author would be glad to hear from any copyright holder whom she has been unable to trace so she can make acknowledgement in future editions of this book.

All Biblical quotations are from the New International Version unless otherwise stated.

My special thanks to Andrew for his love and patience in editing the manuscript and encouraging me.

"For we do not preach ourselves, but Jesus Christ as Lord, and ourselves as your servants for Jesus' sake." (2 Corinthians 4 v 5)

"God can use our story to plant a seed in someone else's heart."

Rev. Don Smith Oct. 2010

Part One

"He breaks me down on every side,
And I am gone.
He uprooted my hope like a tree."
(Job 19 vs.9 & 10. Revised Standard Version)

Chapter 1

It seemed like a good idea. A walk into Haywards Heath to buy some cream cakes for tea sounded refreshing. I had been working in the kitchen of the big house in Sussex for just over three months, but it often felt much longer. I was part of a Community dedicated to bringing in the Kingdom of God through the `poor and needy`, and that certainly had not entailed much time off. So on this particular afternoon, the minute my equally tired friend, Jessica, suggested a break, I agreed immediately. Anywhere beyond the confining four walls would be welcome.

It was in this muffled unattractive state that I first set eyes on my future husband. There were two men in the hall. One was smiling broadly as Jessica gave him directions to the Community office. The other, half hidden in the dark shadow of the ancient chimney piece, was half leaning, half slouching against the wood burner. The thin figure hardly kept himself upright; his gaze was glued to the carpet. It was obvious he did not want to be in our hall. He had long, black, straggling hair. I wondered vaguely if he was another applicant for the Rehabilitation Centre, but mostly I wanted to get outside. Soon the two visitors were on their way to see Jack, the Head of the Community, and Jessica and I stepped gratefully out of the wooden front door. We crunched down the gravel drive, with only a passing remark about the men. Both of us needed some space. God had not told either of us how tough working in a Community like ours would be. Which was just as well.

I had been fearful about working in a Christian Rehab. Centre. I was worried about being with people who frightened me, and with whom I felt I had nothing in common. Yet I did believe that God had called me to be part of that work. I had certainly tested Him. I had pleaded, even wept, but in that last analysis, like Peter, there was nowhere else to go. (John 6:68)

It all felt very strange. Years previously, I had enjoyed the difference of becoming part of this particular Christian community – a charismatic one. I even felt they might be gaining something to their advantage. A good catch really. (I have since repented of pride….) I was a middle class Drama teacher of approximately fifteen years` Christian standing, `born again`, with one year's work in a theatre behind me, and several in Nursery teaching. I was a local Preacher in my Church, kingpin of the Sunday school; and keeping very quiet indeed about a series of depressive illnesses in my `teens, which had robbed me of joy and confidence.

I wanted to forget the psychiatric ward, the endless tablets and the horror of the slow, misunderstood haul to recovery. I worked very hard at forgetting, until God reminded me by calling me to this offshoot of the

Community I had joined. So I moved with the rest of the team into a tumbledown barn of a house near Brighton, and we began to renovate it to hold our vision…a centre for the `poor and needy` to receive the Kingdom of God. We worshipped. We prayed hard. We stood solemnly swearing our allegiance to our cause, in line with Scripture. We were filled with optimism and purpose. How brave we were, but not rooted in practicality, experience, or very much wisdom.

How little we really understood what our calling meant. Through the door came God's selected treasured ones, at a run. Alcoholics, addicts, the emotionally and physically destroyed, the disturbed, the betrayed, the users and abusers of humankind. They broke our windows, desecrated our rooms, and tried our patience. They tested the love we thought we had. They were frightening, demanding, dangerous and mostly ungrateful. They swore, deceived, and destroyed; they stole our privacy and our video recorder. But God commands His friends to love. We tried. The only answer to their needs, and ours, was the Holy Spirit of God, and He supported us in our woeful inadequacy. He knew all about it. Suddenly I was living with people who had only lived before in my head as characters in scripts, and now I was in their play. I helped to run healing weekends during which God turned lives inside out with His compassionate power. He continued to teach me about real humanity, and to show me He needed my weakness simply to speak through. It was a difficult concept. I was jumpy; I was insecure; I became desperate.

"I feel as if I've just landed on Mars. How can I understand how you feel?" I wailed one day to a friendly young lad, an alcoholic, who was helping me wash up the lunch things in the kitchen.

"I don't know," he said truthfully. I didn't know either, and it worried me. I became adept at working hard in the kitchen to hide my feelings of uselessness and fear. There must have been a mistake. Others were supposed to be here, but perhaps I had taken a wrong turn in my Christian walk, after all.

The two men Jessica and I had passed in the hall that autumn day had been in no doubt of their destination. They had come all the way from the North of England, and they were bound by a friendship of mutual trust and understanding. The younger, leaning against the wood burner, was uncertain about our community, too. His name was Steve, he was thirty-two and he was in the middle of drug withdrawal. Hours ago he had been on a hospital ward, safe in a protected environment he knew. Now he was a stranger, in a strange land, and hating every moment.

Steve was used to feeling out of place. He had begun young. According to his mother he was always `difficult`, and had arrived in an agonizing birth five weeks before he was due. As the months slipped into disjointed years, Steve's mother retreated into an affair with the bottle, and his father, a high-ranking Air Force Officer, deepened his relationship with a girlfriend of long standing. At fifteen Steve was the centre of a bitter divorce wrangle. Confused, he spent time alternately with his mother, his father and his father's new wife. Steve wondered who he belonged to, and if anyone valued him at all.

At school he discovered that a feeling of well-being came from solvent abuse, and, as he grew up he was to progress through cannabis to `soft drugs`, and alcohol abuse. At school he was shy and fearful, until he knocked out the school bully in desperate defence, and suddenly acquired a reputation for being tough. He encouraged this to the full, learning, in many ways, to attack first and ask questions afterwards. Attack was the best method of defence he knew, and he had nothing to lose, except his pride.

The young man taught himself to play the guitar, practicing for hours at a time in a cold bedroom at his mother's house. He had talent and it was sharpened and shaped by his determination. He knew he had worth. This was a gift he had cultivated with hard work. He progressed to the electric guitar, becoming part of a rock band in which he achieved a measure of the recognition he craved. But the pull of drink and drugs on his life continued, and he was sacked from the band for inefficiency whilst high on heroin.

The drug began to grip him. His mother, struggling with addiction herself, did her best to help. She persuaded him to try a drug rehabilitation centre.Over the years Steve went through fourteen more, but was unable to break free of his habit. Failure was bitter to him. Determined, he began work as a miner in a coal pit, and soon managed to drink most of his mates under the table, whilst maintaining their respect. At twenty-one Steve became an under manager at the Pit, responsible for a team of men, underground.

His determination seemed to have worked; now he used drugs only occasionally, mainly to relax. He had his own house that he enjoyed improving. He married, and after the tragedy of a stillborn first son, adored the second, a little boy called Lee. Steve enjoyed his job and did it well. He led Pit rescue teams, and his men were fiercely loyal as he could both administer discipline, and become involved in their lives. He was the youngest under-manager in the Pit, and could stay on his feet and work after they became exhausted. Part of this ability was due to determination, and part was due to a gradual increase in drug abuse.

Steve had worked long and hard to maintain the family he himself had never had, but the cost was high. The hours he worked stretched and became unsocial. Secretly he felt he'd been trapped into marriage, and began to spend more time down at the Pit than with his wife. Predictably, she sought comfort elsewhere. Steve, his pride in tatters, tried to kill her lover. Then he divorced her, but lost custody of his beloved son. Now drink and drugs became even more seductive, and he began to fail to turn up for shifts. When he did he was often incapable of work. The Pit had no alternative but to release him, and without a wage he could no longer pay the mortgage on his house. In one year Steve lost his wife, his son, and his home.

He hit the streets with a vengeance, and was soon recruited by what amounted to the Mafia in his northern city. He earned money for his drugs and drink by brute force, menace and skill with his fists. Just under six feet (to his constant annoyance), he became an expert cat burglar, minder, drug dealer and completely merciless fighter. Half his time he was high on alcohol and drug cocktails to blot out his anger and pain, which lent madness to his exploits. The Drug Squad were desperate to catch him, and to make charges stick, but he was too wily. He had an irrepressible sense of humour that could descend to ruthlessness with the speed of blinking. Steve knew all the tricks for vanishing illegal substances, and invented a few of his own. He lived on his wits, and often those of others, without any thought of reproach. He built his own circle of friends on the streets, many like himself, and he had nowhere of his own to live at all.

Steve was with his girlfriend one day, sharing a quiet smoke in a shop doorway, when a man walked up to him and told him Jesus loved him. For the first time Steve found that all his threats and abuse had absolutely no effect whatsoever. The man was called John and he'd come from a background like Steve's own, but he now attended a Christian Bible College. John came back the next day. And the next. He was tougher than Steve and just as powerful physically. He'd been a gangster and a drug smuggler in South Africa, and there wasn't much that frightened him. Eventually, Steve began listening. John invited Steve and his girlfriend back to his home to meet his wife. The couple fed them and talked about a God who loved them. John spent hours with Steve simply talking, and listening to him, night after night. Steve was fascinated. He couldn't leave his life-style, but he couldn't leave John either.

Then Steve became involved in a trial for burglary and was promised an alibi by his brothers in crime. That support never came, and this shook him to the core. A little while after this Steve accepted Jesus as his Lord, and then went and told his Mafia bosses why he would no longer be able to work for them. He expected to be killed. Instead, he was banished from the city on pain of death.

Part of his release from the Courtroom had been the condition that he would attend a Rehabilitation Centre to come off heroin. So Steve overcame his loathing for such places and agreed. It was either that, or a jail sentence. It was the ever-faithful John who located our Centre in the South of England, and drove Steve there from a hospital ward. It was no wonder that Steve looked out of place, standing in our hall. But, like me, he had nowhere else to go.

"I ask Him to strengthen you by His Spirit, not a brute strength, but a glorious inner strength, that Christ will live in you, as you open the door and invite Him in. And I ask Him that with both feet planted firmly on love, you'll be able to take in with all Christians the extravagant dimensions of Christ's love."

(Eph.3 `The Message` Eugene H. Peterson)

Chapter 2

I did not see Steve for days. His emaciated form seemed to have been absorbed into the very house and grounds. Then he reappeared occasionally, briefly, in the Hall or Dining Room, swiftly melting back into the welcoming shadows. I learned he was in the care of Dave, who had once worked with recovering alcoholics at a centre in Scotland. He often searched for hours for his charge who had expertly given him the slip as the time to work approached. I sometimes glimpsed the two men together on the estate, deep in conversation. Once there was a rumour in the kitchen that Dave had sent Steve up a small apple tree in the orchard, fruit picking, and Steve had treated him to a volley of verbal abuse and near attack. I smiled to myself rather uncomfortably, having no idea of the weakness or paranoid terrors suffered by addicts in the midst of drug withdrawal. I didn't envy Dave's task of teaching or occupying this Northern stranger.

As tales of Steve's explosive temper filtered back to the kitchen, I gave this unpredictable man a wide berth, even though he was supposed to be a Christian. The old fear flared in me immediately. It became obvious that Steve was having major problems adjusting to the loving enthusiasm of an evangelical Christian Community, never mind from the angle of discipline. Team members would often wrap each other in a warm hug of fellowship. To a stricken ex-addict this seemed positively intrusive and quite alien to his thinking. Once, as I passed the telephone in the hall, I caught Steve growling down it to his probation officer.

"For God's sake get me away from here...they're all loonies!"

But the lunatic love that God poured through us gradually began to shape a shaky form of trust. Steve and Dave came to prayer and teaching meetings. For weeks they had fierce, monumental arguments, and Dave used every ounce of his being to convince Steve that he was cared for, and valued. They worked together on the estate, pushing sinew and emotional fibre to their utmost. The team prayed. And prayed, as we did for all in the house. Gradually Steve began to put on weight. In the spring, he took over the wood cutting duties for the firewood of the house, keeping the great baskets stocked as the chilly evenings persisted. He became an expert with the chain saw and axe. He read the Bible. John visited often to encourage him, and quieten his fears.

As Steve worked, he grew physically and spiritually more fit, even a little closer to the Community. We discovered the reason he never wore a coat outside was that he didn't possess one. Instantly someone gave him their own leather jacket. He softened. He would come and eat with everyone else now at mealtimes. Steve said little, but watched us all closely, a little like a cornered wild animal. He would eat rapidly and, immediately he had finished his food he would leave the room.He moved as noiselessly as a cat, despite his height. This unsettled me.

I was strangely disturbed by this quiet dark man and his odd behaviour. I felt uneasy when he was in the room, and I couldn't understand why. He and Dave often came to the back door of the kitchen for a mid-morning cup of tea, Steve always silent. I would do my best to be extremely occupied as I had no idea (as usual) what to say. One lunch-time Steve gave me a broad unexpected wink after he'd tasted some soup I'd made. Horrified, I blushed, and fled back to the kitchen.

Weeks later, I was tramping back over the fields from Haywards Heath with some shopping, when, to my alarm, I saw Dave and Steve walking towards me. As I passed them I burbled very brightly to Dave about the weight of my shopping. Steve simply stared at me in silence. Years later he told me he had thought me very `stuck up`, and had to be pacified by Dave. "She has been through a great deal in her life" But at that time, heart banging, I sped over the remaining yards to the house and safety, and anonymity. I was unreasonably frightened, without knowing why. Again I was furious at my inability to relate meaningfully.

It was shortly after this that I met Steve, alone, on the top landing of the house, as I went to walk down the stairs. I hurried again to pass him, being really conscious of the frightful cold sore that had come up on my lip only that morning. Too concerned with image, this special, precious child of God felt very unlovely indeed.

To my astonishment, Steve stopped and peered at me from beneath his dark unkempt hair.

"What you need for that is a dab of shaving lotion." It was a sudden blunt remark, and then he was gone.

"Yes," I gasped to thin air, "I'll try that. Thank you." Thus God brought us together. I fled to the kitchen.

"You'll never guess what" I yelped to Helen, who was patiently stirring a huge saucepan on the stove, "Steve spoke to me." She smiled and went on stirring.

I've never had a cold sore before, or since. I tried the shaving lotion. It hurt…but it worked.

"My bone clings to my skin, and my flesh: and I have escaped only by the skin of my teeth."
(Job 19:20)

Chapter 3

Each evening now I noticed Helen could be found seated at one side of the huge fire in the drawing room, knitting comfortably. Seated opposite her, usually in a clean white shirt and jeans, sat Steve, fresh from his day's woodcutting on the estate. He would be picking out melodies on her battered old guitar. Once or twice I stopped by the drawing room door and listened. The music sounded very good, despite the quality of the guitar.

"That Steve can certainly play." Helen remarked to me with pride, one day in the kitchen. "We just sit there. I think 'e' likes the company, bless 'im'."

One evening I stood a long time listening. The music was quite beautiful, intricate and rich. Eventually, I peered round the door. Steve was alone. The next moment I was warming my hands by the crackling flames. He went on playing, not acknowledging me at all. I was ready to retreat when he stopped.

"Do you mind...?" I asked nervously. He grunted and began playing again. I curled up in the opposite armchair, enchanted. The music had passionate purity, a skill and vibrancy that held me motionless. It was completely at odds with the solid, dark, hunched figure through which it poured. The contrast was bewitching. The music was joyful; a sort of deep singing that personified Christ. I felt caught in a rainstorm of beauty, drenched and breathless when it stopped. I smiled and said that it was 'lovely'. We sat companionably the rest of that evening, Steve playing as I watched the fire and listened.

There were many such evenings. Soon Steve began to risk a few sentences, between tunes. I always replied carefully, defensively, still a little uneasy. One evening I was suddenly aware that I always met him by the drawing room fire. Before I sat down, I said,

"I do hope you don't mind...I'll go if you want to be on your own..." He didn't look up, but the reply was gruff and as strong as his northern accent.

"I was 'opin' you'd come."

And so we began to talk, cautiously, gingerly, about nothing in particular. We enjoyed each other's company. I found myself watching his clever fingers; his arms were now muscular with swinging an axe day after day. I liked his direct no-nonsense manner, and was captivated by the passion of his playing. Eventually he asked if I had a boyfriend, and I was astonished. The truth was, I had been in love with the same man for years but without result; I couldn't see what business it was of Steve's. I was even more surprised at his crisp reaction to my reply. His sense of humour seemed suddenly frozen. Our meetings continued (to the interest of the Community), and I found that I enjoyed being with him, chatting, laughing and sharing his music. Sometime after his question, I suddenly noticed a tattoo on his forearm as he played. It was then as I sped to the urn in the kitchen to make myself a cup of coffee, I thought,

'I can't possibly fall in love with this man, he's got a tattoo.' I faced the fact that I was...and I couldn't halt it. Reality struck. I also realized that I was a snob, which was worse, and that God must be smiling.

In that Northern city, the Drug Squad had waited long for the right circuit Judge to be sitting when Steve was summonsed on drug charges. They had a very good reason: the Judge for whom they waited had lost his own daughter to a heroin overdose. Somehow the very trial date was changed so that this particular Judge would preside. The Drug Squad wanted revenge for years of hoodwinking and failure. Over the months, Dave had driven Steve north constantly for questioning about his involvement with the criminal underworld. The fury of the law reached fever pitch when it was discovered that Steve had repented and become a Christian, stopped taking drugs, and also refused to volunteer any incriminating information about his old associates. Once he was beaten `off the record` with wet knotted towels in a cell, in the police station where the questioning took place. No marks, no evidence. Powerless, Dave drove him south again, almost incoherent with anger.

As the trial date drew nearer Steve became more tense and silent. He knew the judge and his background. By every logical standard he expected to be put in prison for a long time, and he knew he deserved no less. We all prayed daily, interceding for God's mercy to overrule severe judgment. Jack, the Head of the Community, had decided to go to court with Steve and Dave. He wanted to testify to the extent that Steve's life had changed since he had become a Christian, and `a valued member of the Community`. Steve's nerves began to quiver. One day he went missing, and bought and drank a whole bottle of sherry, before staggering back to us at the house, repentant and desperate.

The day of the trial dawned. Before he left, I handed him a card with a smiling yellow face on it; the only yellow face in a sea of smiling faces. I felt he was special now. With typical bravado he gave me a huge wink as he walked out of the front door. I then went and cried, because I thought I would never see him again, and I couldn't understand why that mattered so much. After all, I was in love with someone else.

We all heard about the trial later. When Jack was asked to swear on the Bible in court he held aloft his own Bible, and spoke firmly without reading from the proffered card. His words about Steve were matter-of-fact. He explained clearly that Steve had given up drugs and given his life to Jesus Christ. He was working this out in his actions and commitment to our Community. The Drug Squad sat grim-faced in a line at the back of the court. Steve locked his knees and put on an expressionless face as the Judge eventually came to the sentence. This was the man whose daughter had died of heroin, and before him stood the cleverest ex-heroin dealer the Law remembered. The Judge decreed that Steve's change of heart was `commendable`, and wished him every success in his new life. The sentence was commuted to Community Service, to be overseen by a Probation Officer.

"As Scripture says," the Judge finished, "Amen…which means, 'so be it'."

As Steve walked past the Drug Squad, angry and incoherent at the back of the court, he couldn't resist winking characteristically.

It was outside that he wept at the mercy and grace of God.

"Think not you can direct the course of love, if it finds you worthy, it directs your course."
('The Prophet' - Kahill Gibran)

Chapter 4

"When I came back from Court, everyone hugged me except you." Steve was looking at me in a gruff, puzzled way.

"I know. That was because I wanted to." I explained earnestly. He shook his dark head, feminine logic completely escaping him.

I had stood rooted to the spot in the drawing room as most of the Community hugged him joyfully. He had borne it patiently, smiling, embarrassed, glad of the affection, but shy. We never took our eyes off each other. I saw Stella and Jack exchange a meaningful glance, and I fled to the kitchen.

At our next fireside meeting Steve was more relaxed than I'd ever seen him. He was also more vocal.

"What do you have to do in this place to ask someone out?" he demanded without preamble.

"I...er...don't know. Ask Jack I suppose..." I squeaked.

"Right." With that he put down the guitar and strode from the room. I fluttered and gulped for a while, and then I literally ran to find Stella, Jack's wife. I later learned that Steve was combing the house to find Jack, as I searched for Stella.

I had taken God at His word shortly after I had joined the team at the big house. I had asked Him for what I wanted. I wanted a husband. It was as if God spoke to me then,

"Go in peace, your faith has made you whole." (Luke 8:48)

Rather excited, I wrote to the man I had been in love with for years, fixing a date for his visit to us at the Community. I reasoned that God needed me to supply that helpful nudge in His affairs, and this relationship was destined for marriage. But my intended never arrived.

What happened was that I suddenly had permission to go for a drink at the local pub with a man who obviously had his own agenda about me. I was suddenly faced with a decision. Who was I in love with...? I found the struggle surprisingly difficult, and prayed long and hard. This sort of thing usually happened to somebody else. Then the pattern of years broke. God seemed to like Steve and me together. Amazed, I took the risk. We were joined in our Pub trips by a lively young Alsatian called Carla, deemed un-trainable by her Community owners. Within two months Carla and I were willing, biddable women, and Steve grew almost visibly in stature. Steve knew how to handle dogs because his mother had bred them, and I felt his pedigree with women was just as good. He did seem a little brutal with Carla sometimes, but I chose to ignore that, blinded by romance. So we enjoyed cider together and at crisps, chatted and relaxed in an easy friendship that didn't include touch. (`I didn't want to mess anything up, ` he confided years later.)

This seemed a far cry from the constant rumours of Steve's explosive outbursts of temper. They were terrible. Once he chased Stella round the huge kitchen table with a knife, swearing at her. I stood and shook with fear in the adjoining small kitchen. His temper was sudden violent and terrifying. Yet no alarm bells sounded in my head. Then one evening he shouted at me, and I ran upstairs and cried myself to sleep. This was the end of everything. The next morning, I had the strange feeling that there was a note in my letter pigeon-hole, downstairs. I got out of bed and went to look...There was the note.

"If you want to talk to me I'm fishing down by the lake. Steve." I can still remember my shoes thudding in the gravel of the drive, as instantly I tore out of the house and down to the lake. He didn't apologize, but later he told me that the reason he'd been angry was that he didn't believe I'd ever consider staying with `a villain` like himself. The next day I found a milk bottle full of daffodils placed carefully on my bedside table.

Life was difficult for Steve without the drug culture that he knew so well. His strong will would often clash noisily with Jack who would accuse him of `rebellion`. Steve had survived working out his own ideas, and he found it hard giving them up, submitting to the heavy leadership of others who said they were following God's plans. The Christian culture was one very alien to a worldly Northerner. He was sometimes unwilling to adapt.

"If only we had his will," Jack would say, "what a leader he would make!" The two men pushed each other endlessly, wrestling with practical applications of faith in Christ. Once, Steve hit Jack round the face to see what he would do, and Jack literally turned the other cheek with no retaliation. Coming out of gangland death fights, Steve was cornered, impressed, and moved to tears.

As his confidence grew, Steve's faith grew. I was proud of him as he turned up for early morning prayer meetings, and was obviously working to understand his God, and learn about Him. He was baptised; and confided that once he was completely clear of drug withdrawal, and stronger, he wanted to help other addicts. Two of his addicted friends from the North soon travelled to the Community, and as Steve advised Jack in a practical capacity, the Community interceded for them in prayer. God brought them both off heroin with minor side effects, leaving them the hard work of maintaining this victory. The couple had been addicted many years, their small daughter living in and out of care. This was their decisive start to being completely `clean`. The reality would take work to test it. God had begun. They later settled, as a family, in Brighton, and went on to work in a Christian Centre for rehabilitating drug addicts. Steve bullied them through their own side effects in our Community, in a firm understanding way. I caught a glimpse of God's workmanship I never forgot.

One evening Steve handed me a letter before he went off to play table tennis, in the recreation area which the Community had made in the hall. Few could beat him at this, and he was tremendously proud of his speed and strength. He was almost arrogant, and I was very awed. I sat on my bed in the room that I shared with Helen, and opened the envelope. It was the best letter I have ever read in my life, and I told him so when I went downstairs. He didn't pause in his game as I came down the sweeping staircase again. He told me later that his heart was actually going like a trip hammer, but he kept a casual expression. He sauntered over to me eventually, having won his game.

"The answer is yes please," I said. He simply beamed. He'd asked me to marry him, saying he didn't have anything to offer me, but he hoped to have in the future. His fear of rejection had made him write instead of asking me openly.

I'd decided already. I felt that God was saying to me that He had put His love for me in Steve, and His love for Steve in me (1 John 4:11). I didn't hesitate.

That night the house suffered a power cut, and was plunged into total darkness. In the kitchen, I heard Steve calling me from the yard outside the back door.

"I can't see anything!" I yelled. "I need a hand." Seconds later his hand closed over mine for the first time, and I stepped outside with him into the darkness.

"Set me as a seal upon your heart,
As a seal upon your arm:
For love is as strong as death."
(Song of Songs 7:6 Revised Standard Version)

Chapter 5

Steve was very concerned that I should get married in the white dress I wanted. To begin with, Stella and Jack were concerned that I wanted to get married at all. Such a situation had never arisen before in their Rehabilitation Centre, or the Community from which it had sprung. So a meeting was arranged for Steve and me and the Minister who headed that Community. He was a quiet, humble man with a powerful international teaching ministry, a call to the nations. I had talked with him years previously, when I joined the Community and we recognized my call. I trusted him.

Now, seated opposite him in the quietness of his study, I noticed that he was watching Steve and me carefully. Steve was on the edge of rebellion, uneasy, as he always was under scrutiny. The minister asked us questions, listening intently. I felt he was listening both to God and the couple in front of him.

"Would you ever hit Jenny?" he asked Steve suddenly with great directness. Steve exploded.

"Of course I wouldn't. What do you think I am..?" There was no reply. After a while he prayed with us both, and there came a prophetic picture. I would have cause to remember it.

"I see two trees. One is strong and stout with deep roots. The other is not as strong, spindly, and it is supported by the first. They are growing together."

Everyone in the room drew their own conclusions, including myself.

The minister blessed us. He promised that he would conduct the blessing of our marriage himself, although the actual marriage was to be held in a registry office as Steve had been married before. I was so pleased our proposed union had been `approved`, and in the relief that I, the weaker tree I thought, was gaining support. I chatted away joyfully to Steve later, but he was still smarting from his questioning.

"What do you people think I am?" This was a favourite phrase of his. I tried to bridge the culture gap. At least we appeared to have gained a measure of approval. He snorted. "Wouldn't have made any difference. I'd have run off with you anyway. I don't need anyone's permission!"

"Would you indeed?" I was almost horrified, but flattered. "When did you decide all this?"

"Just after I got here. I saw you, and thought," That's nice, I'll have that."

"You what?" He was grinning now, liking my amazed expression. My whole upbringing of unworthiness and abandonment was waving flags of bewilderment.

"But why me? Stella said she thought you would have gone for Veronica....anyone else really…" He wrinkled his nose dismissively.

"No. You're different. And you've got a beautiful face."

The teenage years I'd spent, ignored by my peer group, unheard, and overlooked as I struggled to rebuild my life after several `nervous breakdowns`, threw a blanket over the minister's startling question. And there were others, too, that sometimes rose to the top of my mind. In the past I had been overweight, unfashionable and jobless because of enforced psychiatric care, and my self esteem barely existed as I began my Christian life. Jesus was the rock on which I could stand faithfully, whatever I looked like, or whatever others thought about me. It was Christian teenagers who gave me my first taste of the accepting love of Christ, and encouraged me to go to Teachers` Training College. His love, through them, believed in me when I couldn't believe in myself. Men, however, were a mystery I couldn't risk.

My ideas were romantic and mainly fearful. I had not been able to accept that I was loved, let alone love myself, or anyone else. So I had found refuge in a long line of `crushes` in which the object of my affections was always impossible to obtain. There was great safety in this attitude. It worked. I wrote passionate poetry instead. Then came the 'crush' I couldn't pass. He wrote poetry too, and a genuinely caring friendship emerged. He became my fantasy figure, and I waited patiently. I was unsurprised and safe when there was no deep romantic involvement. He had even seen my vulnerability and was maddeningly kind and adult. It was at this point that Steve arrived, and hit my emotions like a grenade.

"Would you ever hit Jenny?" What a question!

I prayed and prayed, alone and with others. We were all a little startled at the clarity of what God appeared to be saying. I chose my direction. I couldn't get over the surprise that Steve had chosen me. No one ever had. God had…but He was God.

My great love had returned from University once, arm in arm with a feisty, stunning blonde, and they wore each other's jeans with all the obvious implications. I was deeply impacted. I was shocked too. One of the first things I did, after Steve's and my engagement was announced to the Community, was to find a pair of his jeans that fitted me. To his amusement I wore them with great relish. This was my revenge upon every woman who had acted as if I didn't exist, and possessed what I wanted.

Steve continued to work on the estate. He was still weak in submission to authority and strong willed as ever. Yet he was vulnerable too. His volcanic temper was plain.Not so plain were the hours of Bible reading and prayer. His old leadership skills began to return. He gathered naturally round him a team of men who had come out of slavery to drink and drugs, and were finding a new identity through the Community. Steve was quick to point out, `I'm not out of the woods,` with regard to old temptations, but he edged forward with these men, and they respected him for that. Meanwhile, I continued to work in the kitchen, dreamy and disconnected, often burning the lunch-time soup.

Sometimes, in the evenings, we visited the local pub with Carla. Gradually, as time went on, a slight tension began to creep into our time together. Once or twice there was a row, and desperate tears from me. Steve often looked angry, and was very quiet. The pressure was building for him to meet my parents, and it was something he dreaded, for the vein of rejection ran very deep indeed in his life. The time was fast approaching, too, when he would again have to commit himself to a woman. They generally betrayed him. The last one had taken away his son. Once he asked me outright,

"Would you ever leave me?"

"I'll cling on like a terrier." I replied instantly, meaning it. He grinned.

Yet now his temper was becoming more explosive, and I often caught him watching me carefully, as if I might be planning to cut and run. Tension increased. There were rumours in the Community that he had smuggled the local barmaid back to the house one night. A married woman in the Community began to look at him with what I considered ungodly affection. Steve hotly denied this. He had an incredible naivety which was most appealing. We both began to get irritable.

Steve became deeply suspicious of the evenings I spent with one of my two good friends in the Community. I had to plan times apart to pray with them. He was also very interested and exacting about my past relationships, particularly with men. His great wound of betrayal was far from healed. I didn't realize this at the time, and became quite indignant in the face of his questioning about my past sexual behaviour. He seemed pleased that I was a virgin, a fact he would keep checking with me. A little embarrassed, I put all this down to the eccentricities of men, especially from the north of England, and I felt cherished and feminine. Yet there was real anger in him, almost a fear, when I emerged from a medical check up some weeks before our marriage.

"Did he touch you?" he demanded.

"Of course he did," I wailed, "he's a doctor!"

"You know what I mean…" I felt a twinge of fear that I smothered instantly.

"Of course not," I lied, wondering what was happening. I justified myself by being forgiving, moved by his possessive, protective attitude. It felt good to be wanted, and desired. And I had begun to want Steve, too. And God had given him to me…..

"My transgression is sealed up in a bag,
And Thou dost wrap up my iniquity."
(Job 14:22 Revised Standard Version)

Chapter 6

"They have to get married," Stella told my mother unthinkingly.

"Pardon?" My mother's tone rose down the telephone.

"I mean," Stella said hastily, "they're so much in love. I think the Community will settle more, too, once they marry. It's all been a bit unsettling..."

I went into serious panic a week before the wedding. I couldn't get a responsible answer from Steve about anything, including future work. My parents had not really understood my quiet defensive choice when they met Steve, but they had accepted him instantly. They had been touched by his heartfelt intentions to do the best for their daughter. This was not obvious at the moment. He was becoming seemingly paranoid and growling at everyone, while keeping me under close scrutiny. I was puzzled. An air of unreality was enfolding me like a mist. I knew I was doing the right thing, but it had a taste of inevitability that was almost frightening. I cornered

Jessica as my worry reached its peak, and we sneaked away to pray together.

Jessica was reliable, faith-filled, and a rock of common sense, who went on to become the Chaplain for a young offenders` prison in Suffolk. She also had a marvellous sense of humour. The only private place we could find to pray that day was the dimly lit freezer room, near the Community kitchen. It was not a big room, and I can remember being jammed against the huge freezer and smelling the dust of years, as she faced me over the Formica top. Her pleasant face was troubled.

"Jenny, I don't know what God is doing…"

"What do you mean?"

"Well," she said slowly, "I can feel His pleasure at you and Steve coming together. He is so pleased. I believe He is saying you will be a crown in His hand…" Sheer relief flooded me. I felt the same.

"But what is the matter, Jessica?"

"I'm not sure. He is so pleased. I believe all this is right….I just don't know what God is doing…"

Now, Jack and Stella put the Community into 'wedding mode'. We were promised work and lodging after our honeymoon, and borne to the day of marriage on preparations, invitations, and planning accommodation for guests. I was lent a beautiful white wedding dress and a string of expensive pearls. Steve was completely banned from even a tiny glimpse of my dress. The dream moved on until the appointed day. I had burnt the Community soup for the last time as a single woman. My faith was about to make me whole.

As the sleek white car sped along country roads to our designated honeymoon cottage, my silent bridegroom suddenly leant forward and whispered to the driver.

Three minutes later the car stopped at a garage where Steve jumped out and bought some sweets. I remember this simple, strange act filling my heart with foreboding.

He was quiet and tense as we settled into our borrowed cottage. We were alone for a whole week without the bustle of Community life. I noticed the silence, but was lifted up, wrapped in romantic dreams, and glowing at the promise of my new situation. The cottage was idyllic, beamed and spotless, with pretty patterned matching curtains and furnishings. It was supposed to be old, but was as new as I felt, and I was completely ready to embrace the man and the dream God had provided.

To begin with we were like jumpy friends around each other, and then self-consciously we began the rituals of a honeymoon couple. But there seemed an awkwardness in our closeness, a politeness that warded off passion. A little coy, I decided most honeymooners were probably the same, and was not offended by my groom's lack of closeness. Our first night we simply slept in each other's arms. I was delighted he was so courteous, and felt safe and loved.

During the days, as we walked the surrounding countryside, I gradually became uneasy. Steve was spending much time with me in nearby pubs, and simply listening to music on headphones in the cottage. We would find a pub at opening time, and not leave it until late afternoon. Steve seemed to be in a strange dreamlike state that almost excluded me. I became aware that his mood would go through a range of levels through the day. He was irritable in the morning, silent, then calmer as he downed cider, culminating in a loud arrogance. It took me a little while to work out that he was continually getting drunk.

The warm-hearted, kind man I loved would re-emerge a rather scaring alien, who bore the name `husband`. I sat grimly opposite him at many wooden pub tables, watching the change, angry, frightened, and eager for the Steve I knew to appear once more. I had never experienced anything like this before. He would begin gentle and boyish, his old self, and end angry and argumentative with me, and anyone else who crossed him.

One night, for no reason, Steve began verbally to abuse a tall thoughtful man drinking at our table, in the local pub. I was bewildered by these unreasonable outbursts, and the venom they contained. Steve had never met him before, but I could see and hear resentment, rejection, and anger pouring from him. This appeared to be because of the man's supposedly superior lifestyle and education. I sat mortified, embarrassed, and white lipped. I was afraid, and I prayed and prayed, silently.

Steve changed tack. As his boasting about his achievements reached its height, fuelled by cider and double whiskey, the quiet man offered to drive us home. I kept wondering why he hadn't retaliated to anything the drink had forced Steve to say. Most men would have knocked him into the middle of next week.

The man put us both into his elegant white sports car outside the pub, and began to drive skilfully in an unruffled sort of way, through the dark. I held my breath, and prayed continually.

Suddenly Steve demanded to drive, plainly delighted with the expensive car. Without a word, the man let him.

Coldness gripped my heart. I had never known fear like this before. The car purred and roared, slicing through the darkness, close to the road at a speed it was never created to achieve. I remember thinking how ironic it was that I was going to be married and buried in the same week. Steve was an excellent driver, intuitive and daring, but far, far too fast. He had trained on many escape drives from angry people who were never able to catch him, and he knew how to push a car, and himself, to the limit.I begged him to stop, but I was silenced in no uncertain terms. Then the calm man spoke to him in a normal, almost casual voice, and Steve gave him back his car. We pulled up outside the cottage, Steve now commending the driver. He was noisy and joyful, I was in tears.

To this day I do not know who the man was, or where he came from, why he delivered a crazed young man and his new wife safely home, or why the car did not end up in the nearest hedge. I never will understand, but that night something of the grace and power of God touched my soul. I knew His presence was with me indeed, even if the situations I was getting into, and would be getting into, were horrifying and unlike any I'd ever been in before.

Pub visits dominated the honeymoon, but I kept pain at bay by centering on the times of laughter and unity. Once, Steve bought me a huge steak sandwich as a special treat.

"You should have seen your face!" he would recall lovingly, years later. "I think you enjoyed that the best out of the whole honeymoon!" He wasn't too far wrong. Community food left much to be desired.

Steve seemed far from his normal self, so different from the man I knew. As we walked through local villages I noticed that he always studied the Chemists shops as we passed. I was completely mystified. Once I heard him mutter, almost to himself,

"Well…that's easy. What are they thinking of?"

"What do you mean?" He glanced down at me at his side, and smiled, a little sheepishly.

"I used to break into Chemists once. Dangerous drugs cabinets. That one would have been simple…" I was completely dumbfounded.

"But I'm not thinking of that."

But he was. I learned, years later, that much of his remote, distant, robotic behaviour towards me at that time was because of the cannabis he was eating. Someone had given him some at the wedding reception. It was traditional amongst addicts when they married, Steve explained.

I had never known the sort of behaviour that resulted from cannabis. I just began to think I was unattractive, un-alluring, and that his passion for me had cooled. I even tried seduction, but when there was no response the pain was extraordinary. Our time together slid into frustration and disappointment…and rows. The last night of our stay in the cottage, Steve chose to sleep on the sofa. I lay alone on the big bed in the bedroom, gazing unseeingly at the immaculate fluttering Laura Ashley curtains, my romantic dreams in shreds. I had never felt so alone. Life had become unimaginable. Was this marriage? What next? My husband no longer wanted me; our marriage was still not consummated. What had happened? I lay there without any sort of understanding, feeling that God, too, had left me.

"For the Son of God, Jesus Christ….. Is not 'yes' and 'no', but in Him it is always 'yes'.
That is why we utter the Amen through Him, to the glory of God."
(2 Corinthians 1:19 Revised Standard Version)

Chapter 7

On our return the Community was in the midst of renovating a disused bingo hall in Brighton. The vision was that it should be used as a 'drop-in' ministry centre and for evangelistic meetings in the future. I mixed quite a few tears with the white paint I was splashing on a cracked wall.

"I don't think my husband loves me any more," I sobbed to a kindly Community member. She shushed and comforted me in a well meaning sort of way, but my despair was deep and genuine. It was many years later that Steve was able to share the truth of the situation as it had been then.

He had actually felt very frightened on the honeymoon. He didn't entirely understand the force of the feelings that had propelled him again into marriage. This had only brought deception, pain and loss in previous years. Fear made him angry. It was as if all the injustices and helplessness of the past suddenly overwhelmed him. The fact that I had expressed my love and desire for him simply highlighted his inability to cope. I seemed to be expecting so much, and he was anxious about the future. Suppose I had rejected him physically as a very new young wife? Where would that have left him? Despised and rejected, the odd one out again, where background and experience had left him before. In his past many women had promised love and faithfulness, and then demonstrated the opposite. Even his mother had deserted him when he failed to kick his drug habit. His ability to trust women was barely alive.

On top of this new conflict Steve hated himself for not being able to be the dream husband I had in mind. He could not embrace the hope, love, or future that God had for him. So he fled to the oldest way he knew of blotting out the pain. Alcohol and drugs. At least it worked. Yet God's people saw this as wrong, so they must see him as wrong. He always had been, and now he was again. They were right and holy. His oldest enemy was back with a vengeance.

Our uneasy alliance lurched from one day to the next, with only flashes of former friendship. My only strength was an awareness of the approval of God in our being together. I struggled emotionally, full of repressed pain and anger, to move in my new role as a wife. Physically we were still strangers.

For a variety of reasons no jobs emerged for us from the Community, and worse still, there was nowhere to live. We were told that the promised flat had `fallen through`. The only alternative appeared to be a bed and breakfast room on Brighton seafront whilst the possibilities of more permanent lodgings were pursued. So with my wedding presents and my dreams in storage,

I worked at decorating during the daytime, and keeping my hope and faith strong the rest of the time.

Steve worked fitfully at the Bingo Hall, disappearing for increasing lengths of time no one knew where. He demanded my company and constant presence with him when he reappeared. I began to feel almost like a validation of his worth before this ardent Christian community. Trust was wearing thin. At one point he was accused of taking a toolbox from the building to sell the tools. The box later turned up in a cupboard.

Our own relationship was not faring much better.

"I do wish you could suggest something we could do, instead of saying 'that's a good idea' every time I say something. It's driving me up the wall." At this, I felt even more alienated. His feelings can only be imagined.

When we weren't in various Brighton pubs at night, we were at Praise and Worship meetings. As the vision rolled on its Technicolor way around us, two of the poorest and neediest folk in the town struggled at its centre. I began to see my honeymoon experiences reappear and deepen in desperation and content. I worried as I watched my husband trying to keep in control of him, me, and a situation that started to get worse with each day. Steve was silent and moody. Anger pulsed through his whole frame, and when released through alcohol it distorted his face and body, mind, and actions. I gave him a wide, fearful berth, physically, each night, as he became more unpredictable. No one came alongside either of us. Except God. The odd thing was that the more disturbing our days became, the more firm, quiet peace I would experience within.

"What is it with you?" a Community member asked me, having just met a volley of abuse from Steve. "The

madder he gets, the calmer you become. It's wonderful."
It wasn't wonderful at all. But it was God (Psalm 4:7).

I had no more idea how to cope with a frightened
hurting ex-addict than the people in the Community,
and was far less qualified. Nor had Steve any idea how to
deal with a too-compliant wife. Each morning in my
prayer time I would ask God what I should do. He alone
was firm and reassuring. He was asking me to trust Him.
So I tried. Like Steve, I hated the drab Bed and Breakfast
room we returned to constantly, and I was concerned by
Steve's mood changes and lack of communication with
me. All I seemed to be able to do successfully was simply
be with him, like the faithful terrier I'd once described. I
clung in the streets, in the pubs, in the Bingo Hall, in
that terrible ugly room, and everywhere we went. He
spoke little, moving quickly and silently. He worked
skilfully and then he would go and get drunk. I would
watch as he ironed his T shirt and jeans for each pub
evening, sad and horrified. We couldn't communicate the
pain.

One evening I reached our room before him, I
thought. The room was empty. I pulled the battered old
wardrobe open. His clothes had gone. His black leather
holdall was missing. (He'd long since sold his guitar.) For
a moment a ridiculous hope soared within me. It was
over. He had left me. Numb, I reported back to the
Community, and then simply waited. I had no idea what
would happen next. I assumed that God knew, because
He generally did.

A few hours later, I heard Steve's key in the lock. He
saw me, and looked away, as he came into the room. He
slung the black holdall on the floor. I asked him if he
wanted a cup of tea. He grunted, and sat down on the

bed. He sipped his tea for a while, and I kept very quiet. I could see he was sober, and troubled. So we began to chat about nothing in particular, as was our way, until he said suddenly,

"I tried to go."

"Did you?" My heart suddenly began beating very fast.

"I did...I wanted to leave...all this. Not you...but..." He was on the edge of tears.

"What happened?"

"Well, I thought I'd go back." He named his city."I could cope there you see. But I couldn't leave. I got to the station but I couldn't..."

"But why?...why?" I needed to know.

"I just couldn't leave you. I couldn't do it..." He began to cry in a mixture of anger and frustration, bewilderment and despair. I put my arms round him. We sat together a long time. Through my relief I knew that although he thought this was true, it was the love of God he was powerless to leave.

"Abandonment is not just hanging loose,
It's a letting go.
It is a severing of the strings by
Which one
Manipulates, controls, administrates
The forces of one's life."
(Anon. `Good Friday People` - Sheila Cassidy)

Chapter 8

There were strands of deeper communication between us now, as we both worked through each difficult day. The Community struggled in the situation, but it was their care that found Steve and I joining the lines of people waiting in the local DHSS, for we needed to pay the rent on our bed and breakfast room. There seemed no alternative lodgings. A comfortable, motherly Community member accompanied us as we waited miserably to be seen. She pulled out her knitting as the time dragged on, working steadily and unconcernedly in the grim atmosphere. I felt desperate. I remember Steve's face; a mixture of pride and anger at having been reduced to these circumstances.

Steve still had an uneasy relationship with Jack. It was caught between fury, disappointment and resentment. There was, however, still the desire to be a valued son, a respected member of the Community. So now Jack was attempting to disciple Steve, almost from a distance, as his responsibilities at the Bingo Hall grew, and Steve sensed instantly his disapproval of our emerging lifestyle. The two men met briefly for occasional fraught discussions, their previous relationship beginning to fray at the edges.

As far as they could, they strove to restore their friendship. Steve was sometimes more secure in himself after times with Jack. Sometimes he went straight out and got drunk. He would return to our room long past midnight, completely incoherent. One tension point between the two men seemed to be that our marriage was still unconsummated. Steve felt tortured by failure. On his return in the early hours of one morning, I watched Steve strip, and smother himself in talcum powder. He did this completely unknowingly, calling the powder by a childish name of many years ago. There was something unbearably sad about this attractive man standing naked and childlike before me, completely vulnerable in a totally altered state of mind. Shock and compassion struggled within me. Relating gently to the child, I was able to get him into bed.

It was around this time I felt my gaze held by a card in the Christian bookshop in Brighton, which read, `God grant me the serenity to accept what I cannot change…and change what I can`. I realized that this must be part of my truth. When there were no meetings at the Bingo Hall and we had no money, Steve and I would often spend sane evenings in front of the small portable black and white television in our room. Steve would be fairly silent, but gentle, and sometimes his wicked sense of humour would surface and transcend the misery. We grew closer. We were in this together.

Gradually work for Steve at the Bingo Hall began to grow less, and his explosive temper tantrums increased.

No thought seemed to be given to his feelings of insecurity and rejection. He was `in rebellion`. Predictably, he began to spend as much time as he could in different pubs, sometimes taking me, sometimes not. He frequently spent our rent money. His street craft skills began to re-emerge, and it became a habit to take handfuls of tranquilising tablets to boost the effects of the cider he drank. Again, opposite him in a variety of saloon lounges, I charted the course of his insensibility. It took me a long time to connect the tablets he was taking with the escalating fury of his mood swings and robotic behaviour.

For me then, the company of Jesus became a new reality. I sought His Spirit within me second by second in dimly lit bars, for protection and stability. I took to locking myself in the nearest Ladies` loo, and praying, because I felt completely panic-stricken. I used to just simply pray at the end of an evening that God would get us back to the Bed and Breakfast room safely. Time seemed to double itself during those long painful nights. The hands on the bar clocks crept on as each speedily-dispatched drink increased the danger element in my partner. Before my eyes he would change by degrees into another person, and I grew to recognize each fractional change, as I assessed our safety. Fear held one hand all the time, but God never let go of the other, and we would always lurch unsteadily through the dark streets right back to the B & B door. The nights I was not with Steve I would pray for his safe return. Once, someone found him wandering, senseless, along the sea front. He'd lost one of his treasured Rockport shoes, and it was awhile before he could remember where he lived. Again, he was brought back to his door.

Soon after this, Steve was walking round the streets by day, insensible, as I trotted by his side. I was often very hungry as he didn't eat much, so that the alcohol and drug level in his body would be boosted, and my needs were swept away by his needs. I lost quite a lot of weight, and my wedding ring had to be taken in, Steve commenting on the jeweller's gain in gold. I became quieter, but remained dogged in every sense of the word. One afternoon we ended up on the, then, recently opened nudist beach in Brighton, and waves were not the main attraction. I remember slithering over the huge pebbles to keep up with my husband, frozen in failure myself, as he cast interested eyes over shapely female bodies. My own was, as yet, largely unexplored.

The Community were outraged. The man was being perfectly rebellious. He needed to repent and return to a manageable state. Had he forgotten his commitment to God? So it was amidst this climate, and as a result of a completely altered state of mind, that our marriage was consummated.

My terror, then, of this mindless stranger, was like a long scratch made across the shine of my caresses and romantic attitudes. I remember being stilled roughly, and as I froze, I was unceremoniously heaved out of bed. All I had fell apart within, at that moment. I had tried so hard. I couldn't believe it as my shoulder hit the wooden floor. Numb, I curled up in a blanket in the dilapidated armchair in the room, and cried. Because of his own sense of unworthiness and shame Steve, drugged and desperate, was unable to receive the love I wanted to give. Thoughts of my parents and my home flashed across my mind. As the thoughts appeared, so too did a picture of a brick wall. It filled my mind completely, and I knew that

God was blocking that avenue of escape. There was a movement from the muffled, tortured mound on the bed. Old fears had overcome him. He was in hazy misery.

"I am sorry...I am sorry..."There was a silence in the dark room.

"It's difficult for me too..." This was an effort, to be vulnerable, appear weak. I sensed something in his suddenly coherent voice, and it pulled at my heart. He too was in pain.I got back into bed.At the worst moment, pain filled, naked, and uncomprehending, out of the nothingness words came into my head;

"Who shall separate us from the love of Christ? Shall tribulation, distress....nakedness...," and I knew their truth.

The new basement flat smelled of damp. It was dark and there were hideous plastic roses in vases on the walls. The door from the tiny kitchen opened on to a small enclosed courtyard, in which was a round white plastic table and chairs. The place had all the charm of the underworld, but the Community were pleased with their efforts.

Another new acquisition was an American worship leader at the Bingo Hall, who was on the lookout for a new guitarist. The idea was that if Steve gave up his wild ways he would be allowed to play in the music team. Steve reacted with disdain and sarcasm, and I simply ached at all the lack of understanding and perception in the whole situation. He was a good musician, but terribly hurt and unsupported, and being obviously manipulated into a form of behaviour that was impossible for him to achieve, at that time.

The musician was demanded, not the man. He needed someone to understand the situation from where he stood, to come alongside him, to present a firm discipline of grace, not law. He needed mercy, not judgment. Steve needed accepting, but the Community understood God's framework as repentance and adherence to a narrow set of rules.

I hoped on hope for some turnabout miracle on Steve's side or on theirs, some breakthrough that would enable Steve to set his will to respond. (For I had trusted these people to oversee my Christian life), l but I was deeply disappointed when he was unable to grasp what appeared to be a redeeming offer of rescue for us both. I was puzzled, too, by this reflection of what stood for God's heart. I looked for compassion, and saw only legality. Bitterly, Steve chose to turn away, and I was consumed with a sadness and bewilderment. I could only take it to God. In Him there was no condemnation.

Smarting from what he saw as betrayal and manipulation, Steve missed meeting after meeting with the earnest Worship Leader. He then coped with self hatred and failure in the only way he knew worked. A new and greater terror became added to my dreads...vodka. One night he drank a whole bottle neat, and I watched him slide down our shabby courtyard wall into a crumpled heap on the ground. It was like a frame in a film, but quite real. What had been outside my experience was beginning to be within it. But there was another reality too. A sense of God's presence, an invisible holding, embraced and protected me, sometimes almost tangibly, moment by moment. It was like being wrapped in warm, white silk. As I remember, more frames in the film flood back to my mind; the Hare

Krishna devotee whom Steve invited to the flat one day. He sat cross-legged on the floor eating vegetables and explaining his devotion. The next morning we found a single rose on the doorstep. A week later, there was of course, an invitation to a Krishna meeting.

"No," Steve said thoughtfully, "I can't go to that. It's not right." Quietly, God was claiming the ground that belonged to Him.

I remember, too, walking into the flat one day to find Steve brandishing a large bottle excitedly. It was full of emerald green liquid.

"Everything's going to be all right now!" He seemed elated. I couldn't understand it at all. The contents of the bottle disappeared during the course of the evening, along with Steve's sanity. A slobbering wreck of a man telephoned my parents, and demanded money from them, as I stood weeping and terrified beside him. Being a registered addict Steve had simply gone to the nearest doctor and used his manipulative expertise to obtain heroin substitute. It opened the jaws of hell to four people. My father was troubled for weeks after that call. I could not explain this away.

Winter dusk was closing in on the long row of terraced houses in the road on a hill, miles from the Brighton seafront. We had been moved from the flat, as the Krishna devotee had reappeared with a drug pusher friend. Now, the inevitable bed and breakfast room waited for our return. It was cold, and fog moved slowly in the orange street light outside the front door. Steve was fumbling in his jeans pocket for the key. I was momentarily prayerful; we had made it to our front door, after a tour of new pubs. He grumbled unsteadily as he hauled the key free, and jammed it into the lock. There was something about the tone of the complaints and threats that suddenly made me grin. I looked up at him.

"You know, you're not really fierce at all are you?"

"I am," he snarled, wrestling with the door. But I could hear the amusement and gladness in his voice. I understood. An image came.

"Dragon!" I said triumphantly. He took the key from the door and smiled down at me. Then he caught his lip in a ridiculous tooth-held growl, and his fingers became sharp claws held up in mock menace. The image of a soft-hearted dragon trying to be fierce was complete, dark hair falling comically all over its face. He had caught and accepted the truth of the remark. And God could see his heart, for that is where He looks, unlike men. We climbed the stairs to our room that night, muddled with unaccustomed joy.

James: "He's wicked I tell you, he drinks…and swears…gambles…"
Jesus: "But do you love him?"
James: "Yes".
('Greatest Story Ever Told')

"For Thy sake we are being killed all the day long;
We are regarded as sheep to be slaughtered."
(Romans 8:36, 37 Revised Standard Version)

Chapter 9

I could see a park out of the window, the railings running down the steep hill, and in between the houses trees pushed leafy branches towards the sky. Now it was the beginning of summer, but already the weather was hot. We kept the heavy sash window of our Bed and Breakfast room open most of the time. Often the sill was draped with jeans and T-shirts drying in the sun.

Recently, a bid by the Community to tame Steve had failed. Protesting about the rights of a man to stay with his wife, he had been taken back to the old house days before in an attempt at detoxification. The next morning, in desperation, Steve had hidden on the floor of the minibus which brought people back to Brighton to work at the Bingo Hall. I had been able to take a few gulps of peace before I heard his footfall on the stairs. Old tensions began within as he opened the door, grinning broadly.

"Hello," I said, masking my disappointment, "what are you doing here?" He dropped on to the bed, and lay flat on his back.

"No way was I staying there. I couldn't stand it. Had a word with Pete. Don't give me away, mate. I want to go back to my wife. Good bloke, Pete. Drives that van a dream…"

The frustrated Community drifted self-righteously a little further from our lives. We would rise late, and either go straight to a pub until afternoon closing, or sometimes take a walk along Brighton Pier. (There was a bar at the end of it.) I used to be knotted inside with the expectation of some catastrophe, but loved the pier from childhood holidays with my parents. It seemed like a point of stability.

The couple who owned the house in which we rented our room were kindly but firm. Mrs.Wilberg, a stout, matronly, part-Jewess, often met me briefly in the back garden, as I used her washing line.

"That 'usband' of yours….be careful 'e's' a naughty boy…just a boy…"

She took to regarding Steve like an errant son, as he stumbled and thudded up her carpeted stairs late at night, drunk and tired. There came to be a warm respect between the two of them, for she did not hesitate to lay down house rules.

As soon as our cheque arrived each fortnight (we were now part of the survival system), we would usually set out for the local supermarket, armed with Steve's faithful black plastic holdall. He had cooked for himself for some years after his divorce. I had not learned much about cooking at all. I disliked it and was largely uninterested. The result of this was that I couldn't cook with any degree of efficiency at all. My weakness provided us with another bond. Steve would often cook our meals, teaching me as he went. To my immense surprise he was both a discerning shopper and a very good cook, painstakingly taught by his grandmother as a boy. Steve remembered her with great affection, especially her accepting love. His family were scornful of him as he succumbed to drug addiction in his teenage years.

"Went to see her...gran...when she was in hospital the last time," he told me once, "and they were all there...round her bed...for what they could get. I'd bought her this pot of violets. She liked those, you see. It wasn't much. They all said, 'Oh, it's only him.' They weren't pleased to see me at all, but she was. 'Hello, lad.' she said. 'Let him nearer.' They hated that! She always used to say to me, 'God is good lad, God is good...'" I often thanked God for this glimmer of Himself in Steve's life. It had burnt deep within his mind and heart.

Our trips to the supermarket were far from good. Steve walked swiftly, looking dark and angry, snapping at anyone who crossed his path innocently, or bumped into him. I walked as fast as I could to keep up with his long strides, cringing inwardly. I was quite unable to understand this seemingly meaningless aggression. I worked on the principle, in these early days, that the best policy for me was to be quiet and compliant. I sensed a deep suffering in this tall, powerfully built man that was erupting in growling outbursts of bad temper, but was unable then to understand its source. Looking back, I imagine the temper was probably based on fear and alcohol withdrawal; perhaps drug withdrawal, too. For sometimes Steve was 'scoring' (obtaining illegal drugs) on his night wanderings, but the effects of these drugs, and withdrawal symptoms, were quite alien to me. His desperation was finding expression in familiar comforting ways.

One morning, in my quest to be the perfect wife, I volunteered to do the shopping alone and meet him later. I decided to choose mainly cut price brands of tinned food so that we could save some money, and looked forward, in a pleased sort of way, to the praise and commendation I thought I deserved. But this day was a particularly bad day for Steve, for any number of reasons I knew nothing about, and we plunged into a furious row as we carried the shopping home after our pub rendezvous.

I had not known that the addictive personality is very prone to routine, especially an enjoyable one such as favourite foods. Food is usually a forgettable necessity, but now, trapped in the small routine of domestic duties, in a completely foreign town, away from familiar friends and security I had taken away his remembered pleasure: good, needed food. Steve had been denied the support of a group of people whom he had begun to trust; denied dignity, and denied freedom. Inwardly he was unbearably frustrated by his own shortcomings, and mine. Steve lost his temper badly. It wasn't altogether about the wrong tins of food. Suddenly he threw the heavy holdall down on the pavement, and hit me hard round the face without any warning at all. Then he stormed off up the road shouting abuse. I was completely numb and in shocked disbelief. I'd never been called such names in my life. Or been hit so hard. `Would you ever hit Jenny? ` As my face began to pound, all I could think of was getting to the Bingo Hall for some help, running to imagined safety. The minister's prophetic question before our marriage was now reality.

I struggled to Jack's office, and there were some people there having a meeting. I opened the door and asked if someone would pray with me, and then burst into tears. When I looked up, one man had tears rolling down his face, too. As I remember, the people there held my hands and prayed with me before one drove me back to the Bed and Breakfast house.

Steve was sitting in our room, strumming a borrowed guitar with great concentration. He didn't look up as I came in, so I put the shopping down, and went to fill the kettle.

"I didn't think you'd come back." There was a great weight in his words. He put the guitar down, and lay on the bed.

"Well, I did." I was being matter-of-fact, anger not too far away.

"Why?" he asked apprehensively. I took a deep breath and crouched down by the bed, near his head.

"Love you." This sounded a lot stronger than I felt. He suddenly put his arms round me, and we stayed there awhile.It was a good feeling. Thoughtfully, he watched me a bit later, as I made the tea.

"You'll need a bit of make-up," he said at length, awkwardly. Puzzled, I glanced in the mirror. I had a multicoloured left eye.

There was a part of my day, a time when Steve was absent, that had become more vital to me than consciousness itself. It was then that I was able to sit down quietly with my Bible, and a small red notebook.I had learned in my Christian life to give God some space, to pray, and to try and catch the tone of His voice. I had come to recognize this as distinct from my own inner turmoil, and now I knew there was a power intimately involved with my struggles each day, and with Steve's. Now I felt God was saying that I was not to be afraid, but to keep allowing His love to flow through me to my husband. He loved us, and He was working in our lives to achieve His purposes. It was I who had covered my eyes in horror after my honeymoon experiences. God was gradually unlocking my fingers and gently lifting my head. It was the strength and peace seeping into me during my precious times alone with God that began to rebuild my fearful mind afresh, and bring me hope. No-one else could do this. I deliberately kept my elderly, ailing parents in ignorance of my troubled life. One disruptive Christmas visit to them had decided me on this point. I worked hard at maintaining worry-free news bulletins. The Community drifted further from both of us, baffled and shocked. It was only the sense of God and His words in a small notebook that ministered love and direction.

We had been given a beautiful duvet and duvet cover as a wedding present, and I'd determinedly kept this within reach. My longing to be 'properly' married, with a home, bubbled and rattled beneath our painful circumstances. Other couples I had known had created their own living space; matching towels, round framed photographs on the walls, a carefully created haven that spoke of their togetherness and safety; a unity of taste and expression. How I envied them. One very warm summer day, I looked round our clashingly decorated room, with the ugly cream mantelpiece, and the brown wooden wardrobe, and I hauled out our very own duvet and matching pillowcases. I pushed the duvet into the lovely pastel cover with great force. Halfway through the night, Steve began muttering and thrashing about beneath my prized possession. He had not said a word about it earlier, as I proudly displayed my handiwork, except to grunt in a dismissive way. Now was different.

"What is the matter with you, woman?" he roared in a flurry of duvet. It sailed upwards like a heavy cloud.

"But....it's our wedding present..." I whimpered, "I thought you'd like it..." There came one of the deepest sighs I have ever heard, a northern man battling for emotional control.

"It's fine," he managed at length, flinging his side off him furiously, "but not, you daft woman, in the middle of bloody summer!" Wounded, I curled up clinging to my side of the cover, loath to admit I was hot, too. I had failed again.

"And lo, I am with you, always…"
(Matthew 28:20 Revised Standard Version)

Chapter 10

Many days we had no money at all. This meant no alcohol and no drugs for Steve, and very little food for either of us. Yet long evenings were shortened by Steve being creative with the provisions we had, and producing surprisingly good meals. They became a focal point. He would concentrate on these to lessen cravings, and to give to me. So we'd sit and watch the black and white portable TV for hours, until it was time to eat.He would be silent. I would be anxious, often wondering how to communicate. These could be quite lonely times for both of us... Black depression would often totally envelop Steve, and he was set almost like stone in the silence. Yet one of the first glimpses I got into his sense of comedy was through an advertisement for soup on the television. The advert depicted a donkey who 'spoke' the word 'thistles' when asked to choose between soup and thistles for supper. With great elegance and precision, technical wizardry had the animal speak the word 'thistles'. This obviously appealed to Steve, so, unbeknown to me he studied the sound and tone of the word each time the advert appeared. One night, in response to my questioning about our food, he gave a perfect imitation of the donkey's reply. I was reduced to helpless giggles. It was so accurate. Thus the advert became a bridge for communication between us. We'd grin delightedly at each other when it appeared, tensions forgotten.

I enjoyed watching Steve prepare our meals; he was always proud and pleased when I consumed them with relish. I tried to learn more about cooking, but my enjoyment came from affirming him. Once, as I watched him preparing meat, I asked idly,

"What is your most favourite meal in the world?" He paused thoughtfully as he placed a piece of belly of pork to cook. Then his face lit up.

"Pig meat," he smiled, nodding at the meat. He wiped his hands on a cloth a moment, and then pointed at me with a grin.

"Pigmeat…!" This made me laugh, and he was very amused, but the name stuck. From then on his name for me was 'Pigmeat', with its range from 'Piggy' to, very tenderly, 'Piglet'.

Faith does not prevent feelings of fear, and fear was always snapping at my heels. When in the grip of alcohol or street drugs, Steve continued to be completely unpredictable, I found myself caught between bewilderment and second guessing every move in case I was harmed.

Day and night, as we toured our established route of local pubs, when finances allowed, I learned to trust God more and more. I made an effort not to look at my fear, but at the man opposite me across endless pub tables.

They seemed to stretch to infinity. I learned to like cider and blackcurrant. Steve became calmer, and we were just part of the moving pattern of life on the street. As he relaxed and became free, I found I could cope, my great anxieties became dulled, and I was open to listen. I watched and listened with everything I had. We joked; we talked rubbish to each other. We invented thousands of different ways to cook seagulls. We tried out different accents; we talked and talked. But the most important part was the listening. In that I both heard and experienced the presence of God with us.

Stories from Steve's past began to tumble from him. I listened to tragic years. The remarks about him, to him, against him, all he'd never quite forgotten turning in his mind to challenge the truth of his own identity. As a boy he had been beaten often, as his mother lost her fight with alcohol addiction. But the child had an ally.

"Gran knew. She'd say to her daughter, 'I know what goes on, don't think I don't. I know what you do..' " Steve smiled gently at the memory of his Gran. "..and....she`d cook me nice meals..." After his parents` divorce, he would often arrange to meet his father. I heard once how the ten-year-old waited for hours wearing his new school mac., outside Marks and Spencer.

"Dad said he'd come, so I waited. And waited. But he didn't come. When I told him later, he said he had forgotten." On the heels of this Steve would be reminded of his own son, and wonder if he would ever come looking for him.

When he did remember to meet his son, Steve's dad would often meet his girlfriend too, by arrangement.

"They'd meet at the railway station where Dad was collecting me, Piggie... as if by accident, and we'd all go out for the day together. But I knew..."Steve was obviously caught between loving and hating his father, and it was a struggle I was to witness many times.

I began to piece together that the beginning of addiction for Steve at fifteen, through solvents and shoe polishes, was a welcome distraction from the feeling of being unloved. So in the impersonal bar space of countless pubs, I'd hear fragmented tales of rejection and abandonment, mingled with anger and rage. I found, over cider-slopped tables, that there was a world I knew nothing about. One in which betrayal and pain were commonplace. And it grew darker still with Steve's 'Mafia'career. This was interlaced with drugs, violence and repressed self hatred. The fighter who was never beaten earned money, esteem, and affection, of a sort, from his 'Mafia Father'. It was in this environment that Steve's mighty tolerance of drink and drugs of all kinds was expanded, and his skills at street survival were shaped and honed. All was driven by fear, shame, and a vast self-loathing.

It was then that I glimpsed the child, trapped in a grown-up body, crying in an agony of pain and longing for all that he had never known. I saw him rendered senseless with drink many times, the very tool he was trying to use to grasp self-respect and well-being. No wonder Steve was unable to accept or see anything good in himself; very few people ever had. As tales of the Northern drug culture jerked and stalled with the Bacardi and cider, I saw a form of acceptance and identification that had welcomed a lost young man. He had embraced that code of living; the people, their rules, their music, and their deaths, to become an undisputed leader here also.

Yet Steve grew angrier still. He was fearsome to cross as his mind became changed by hungry, dark forces. Yet glimmers of light held them at bay. He had broken the rules and summoned help for a dying addict; he had spent money on food for the hungry; he had given where he could not afford it, and cried when no-one had seen. As I listened to the adventures of this prodigal son, my heart ached. I viewed the use and abuse of a vulnerable human being, by a world intent on money, self, and its own mean spirit. I wanted to weep at the result, a man broken and half mad, in part through choice, but whose mind and body were now slipping on the edge of complete destruction.

"Can you imagine," Steve asked me one day during a heated discussion, "living without your Bible?" Emptiness opened up beneath me. For a moment I couldn't. Drink and drugs were this, to him. God had claimed him; now He needed to change him.

"Would you leave me, if I went back on to heroin?" Steve demanded wildly one night.Fear rose and began choking me.

"It's hardly the ideal start to a marriage," I managed dryly; "but, no…I don't think I would…"I could see he didn't quite believe me. After all, a woman had left him before.

Brighton seemed very dark at night. The nights I didn't go out with Steve, I found it impossible to stay in our room all night waiting for his return. Worry and fear would lend wings to my feet. I would run over the dark pavements, past grey shops and houses, only pausing to peep round pub doors, searching the smoky brightness for the familiar face. From pub to pub, from street to street, and once as I ran, my mind fully occupied, a picture from somewhere else began to form in my head. Soon it filled me. It was of a tall man walking along, and by his side gambolled the most beautiful Dalmatian dog, without a lead, but in perfect obedience to his master. I knew the man was Jesus, and the joyous dog, Steve. There were words with the picture.

"I will heal your husband." God's words that night became the hope upon which I stood for the rest of my married life.

"Who shall separate us from the love of Christ?"
(Rom.8:35 Revised Standard version)

"I don't think anyone is normal really….
Not deep down in their private lives.
It depends on a mixture of circumstances…"
('Private Lives'/ Coward)

Chapter 11

The very peak of the emotional and spiritual anarchy came when Steve was arrested, and put in Lewes prison on remand. His story was that he had tried to stop a heroin deal happening on Brighton seafront. The police promptly thought he was the dealer. It didn't help matters that he was 'stoned' (high on cannabis), and quite drunk at the time.

"You see, Piggie," he explained to me, later, "I thought that lad is going to have his life ruined...look what the stuff has done to me!.. I couldn't bear it..."

I begged a car and driver from a suddenly reluctant Community, and went twice to Lewes prison. The first time a supportive John was able to come with me, instantly loving and caring for both Steve and myself. I remember, oddly, how attractive I thought Steve looked in his blue prison shirt. The world seemed upside down. He seemed wild and disorientated. And he kept asking for Jack.

"Why are you smiling?" he asked me once, in a miserable voice.

"Love you…" I said, really meaning it. He looked as if he didn't believe me at all.

The second visit he seemed calmer, but anxious to see Jack, who eventually went to visit him once before the court case.

In Court I found myself in the witness box, strangely reminding me of a pulpit. It was only by recalling my distant Local Preaching days that I had the breath or courage to speak. As I was his wife, Steve was bound over into my care and released. Away from the public gaze he sobbed on my shoulder. Apparently his solicitor was impressed by my performance, but, recovering rapidly, Steve scolded me gently. I should have spoken louder in Court. But I knew that it was only by the grace of God I was able to speak at all.

The Community were badly rattled. Suddenly, a flat became available in a completely different area of Brighton. Our room-shaped nightmare receded, and a more home-shaped space became ours, far from the dangers of the sea-front. I felt dazed and battered emotionally, as we were moved in amid positive comments that rang hollowly in my ears. I had begun to feel like a traveller; there was safety in the place I knew. I felt unsupported by men. The only place of real safety I had was the time that I made in each day with God. Before the Court case He had shown me that He had a firm hold on both Steve and me, and He would not hurt either of us. He, and no one else, was in control of our lives. I sensed this, especially as I was able both to stand up in Court, and speak with the right words. The words actually had the same strength which mine had in a pulpit, the same sound, that I knew wasn't everyday speech. They had not been totally mine. I knew that because I knew my own voice. So I had no doubt God was carrying His children, even if they felt alone, and a little desperate.

At our new flat, life began to assume a familiar pattern, regulated by the amount of money that was available. I can vividly remember Steve hanging out of the large sash window in the lounge, early one morning.

"What are you doing?" I asked, coming into the big shabby room with our breakfast mugs of tea.

"Looking for the postman..." he replied, unmoving for a moment. It was 'benefit cheque' day. We had finished our last food up the night before, and he was looking forward to a drink.

Our mutual sense of off-beat humour was beginning to provide a hidden strength to our relationship, as was our enjoyment of special food when we could afford it. The previous night I had been anticipating a sober, skilful man making the most of the remains of our food store. I knew there would be an element of culinary magic involved. But as we finished watching a favourite TV programme, Steve suddenly leant forward, looked at me and said,

"Get to bed, you," with a perfectly straight face.

"What!" I cried, as he switched off the TV to emphasize the point, "certainly not!..."

"I said...get to bed..."

"But ...but...what about my supper?" I entered the game. He looked innocent.

"What supper? You're not having any supper".

"I am."

"You're not. Bed!" He pointed to the lounge door, pretending to look stern. By this time I was in the role of a child, and enjoying myself, my drama training surfacing rapidly.

"No. Shan't!"

"I'll have to put you to bed, then." He got up.

"You wouldn't dare!" I squeaked, horrified and delighted both at once. But of course he did. I was swept up, struggling and kicking, bursting with laughter and fury, carried to the bedroom, and put to bed fully clothed. He tucked me in carefully, and went, closing the door firmly behind him. I lay and laughed until my ribs ached. Then I crept out, and back up to the multi-paned lounge door. Steve was preparing supper in the kitchen. I pressed my nose against the glass and watched. Then I noticed his slippers near me. When he turned, he saw a tragic face, nose to the glass, holding his slippers in mock submission. He roared with laughter and came to open the door. I was often `sent to bed` after that, and the ritual somehow deepened the bond we now had. There was deep joy between us that we understood each other, and could still have fun in the middle of our difficulties. God had put two children together who needed to play.

Members of the Community would sometimes come to the flat now, to 'talk' to Steve. Gently, firmly, invitingly, they attempted to make him see that he was stepping out of the ways of God. But they always set many conditions for a return to grace. Hurting and angry, Steve was aware of their lack of acceptance of him, however carefully it was hidden. No-one worked at making a relationship with him for who he was, and I felt I heard God insisting that Steve's argument was not with Him. It was with man. He seemed to be emphatic that

Steve was His responsibility, not mine, or anyone else's. Yet I longed for the human touch we both so much needed. John had been called back to the North to home and family, and Jack was becoming daily more preoccupied with the running of the Bingo Hall Centre. Steve missed Jack desperately. As ever, part of him wanted to please him. He would often travel into Brighton and sit near Jack's office, waiting for the chance to see him. He was too proud and unsure of himself to ask Jack for 'an appointment'; too much water had gone under the bridge, and he was frightened of rejection. At length I grew tired of seeing this beaten man clinging to his pride. It was almost worse than the loud drunk. I went to see Jack myself, and outlined Steve's great need for communication, relationship and, above all discipling. Jack said that Steve could talk to his deputy at the Centre, who knew him. I lost my temper.

"But it's you he knows well. It's you he needs. Can't you see that?"

"I don't have time, Jenny. He needs to make relationships with other people. He needs to stand on his own two feet".

"I know that! But he needs help. Can't you help him?" I left the office unheard, uncomforted, and very sad.

Weeks later the Minister who had founded the original Community, and blessed our marriage, was invited to speak at the Bingo Hall Centre. Some were surprised when he told the Community that they were picking up needy and desperate people like stones, seeing all the mud on the stones, and replacing them again on the ground. This was not the heart of God.

There were now many people struggling alone in bed-sits, flats, and squats, without the adequate support and discipling that was needed if they were to be able to come through their old problems. They had been offered Christ...and let down by men. Many returned to their old patterns of life, crime, drugs or alcohol. In the worst cases some chose suicide as the way out of their pain. But by the mercy of God, Steve and I at least had each other and God's love encompassed our struggles.

"Because he cleaves to me in love,
I will deliver him:
I will protect him, because he knows My Name.
When he calls to Me, I will answer him,
I will be with him in trouble….."
(Psalm 91:14, 15)

"We did not want it easy, God, but we did not contemplate that
it would be quite this hard, this long, this lonely."
(Anna McKenzie)

"Who shall separate us from the love of Christ?"
(Rom.8:35 Revised Standard Version)

Chapter 12

We battled on. Steve seemed unable to relinquish his old lifestyle for the new. To him that seemed to demand impossible conditions, which, if he could not meet them, entailed the punishment of being excluded from fellowship with believers. I agonized in prayer. I saw a picture of Steve in my mind as an impossibly wild stallion, bucking and kicking on the end of a long rope. The man holding the other end of the rope was shortening it imperceptibly all the time, yet allowing the horse room. As before, I knew the man was Jesus. Indeed, Steve did still acknowledge Jesus, often to the surprise of the people he drank with. But he was pulling madly from Christian values, perhaps from fear, perhaps from a sense of disappointment and betrayal. Now it was Jessica alone who visited us whenever she could.She and Steve were friends, often having discussed life and spiritual matters at the Community. They respected each other and she was beloved by us both. Steve would always make sure he was at home and sober when she came, And he would cook us all a large, delicious meal.

A few days before we had left our cramped room and Mrs. Wilberg, Steve had remarked to me that he had 'a bit of a cough'. I was very surprised the next day to see him swallowing a whole bottle of cough linctus in two gulps. Now I caught him doing the same thing at the new flat, and started asking questions. Then, rather shame-facedly, he explained to me about the element in the cough mixture that mildly altered the senses.

I began to become more uneasy as the bottle a day consumption continued, yet he was always calmer and more relaxed after the mixture, especially as he often combined it with lunch time sessions at the pub. And then the morning came I dreaded. He awoke depressed and lethargic, and not moving from the bed, he asked me to go and buy him the daily dose. I took the money and walked from the flat with a whirling mind. My Christian sensibilities were completely outraged. It was one thing Steve getting drugs for himself; it was quite another for me to do it for him. I wondered if I should have refused. To me at the time, bottles of cough linctus struck me as more 'wrong' than drinking nightly, or even street drugs. It seemed so obviously, openly, using a drug for a wrong purpose. I suffered an agony of indecision as I walked to the shops. Perhaps I was betraying my beliefs, myself, Jesus, or even adding to Steve's discomfort in the long run? Before I reached the Chemist's shop, I saw a large grey church ahead. I stepped inside and walked up the gloomy side aisle. Peering around, I suddenly saw a life-sized crucifix to my left. So, caught in the middle of an emotional torment I couldn't resolve, I knelt at Jesus` feet, and cried. I knew the pain of the man on the cross had more than absorbed mine, and looking at the silent, eloquent agony, I felt He understood. As my tears slowed, there came to mind the picture of a blind man, tapping along the road with a white stick. Then I suddenly knew that the daily medicine was Steve's 'white stick'. With great relief, I wiped my face, and went to the chemist's shop, no longer feeling that Steve or I was under condemnation, but we were understood and accepted in our weakness.

During these days, we would get up around mid-morning and, money permitting, be in a pub from opening time to closing time in the afternoon. Often pub acquaintances would be invited back to the flat where the drinking would continue. Later we might watch the TV or a video until evening opening time. Steve would begin to prepare purposefully for his night out, whether I was accompanying him or not. It was important to him to have clean, ironed, fashionable clothes and shining shoes, and he went to great lengths to achieve all this. Or, of course, I did, now understanding a little about how he was feeling mentally, or sometimes physically. There were times when I found this lifestyle unbearably difficult. The pain, the boredom and the loneliness were crushing. It was a matter of survival for us both, and perhaps for many of the people we met; yet we both tried to give them what we could. I found that mainly that was time, and acceptance.

Often it was a relief for me when the front door finally slammed, and I was alone. There was peace, and absence of pain. I could not change the situation at all; but I could pray, when I had tidied up the debris of the day. How often I dreamed of a tidy clean white flat as I rounded up ash, coffee cups and rubbish...and of peace.

Now, as I write I sit peacefully in the tidy, clean, white flat that is God's gift to me. Then, I dreaded the sound of the key in the lock.

"Come on, man…come round to my place. We're Christians…my wife won't mind…." But actually I did mind more as time went on. And I minded terribly being left alone when Steve went out some mornings. The aloneness and fear was overwhelming.

"Don't leave me…please," I cried after his retreating back one day. He turned and looked at me in a sort of angry, desperate guilt.

"What do you want me to do?"

I didn't know.

Steve continued to go to the beach some evenings and smoke cannabis with a gang of young men. They eagerly gave him hero status from the stories of his past experiences with drugs, and were equally touched that he chose to spend time with them. When he had been in prison, God had been quite firm with Steve, about leaving me behind on these evenings, and now he was eager that I should join him, if I wanted to. But I didn't want to. I mentally drew back from anyone who 'used drugs'. One afternoon God spoke to me quite unmistakably as I prayed.

"Do not despise them." I heard very clearly. After apologising to me for his behaviour, Steve would ask me, each time he prepared to go to meet them, if I wanted to come. The next time he asked, I agreed. He looked both surprised and delighted.

With beating, anxious heart, I went to the sea front to meet Kev and `the boys`.The pebbles crunched beneath my sandals as Steve and I walked from the beach-side pub clutching our glasses of cider. There was a small group of lads sitting together on the stones watching the sea in the evening sunlight. One looked up and greeted Steve with warmth, but he gave me a suspicious look.

"This is my wife, Jenny," Steve said, "she's all right." All the young men jumped up politely straight away, and shook my hand. The note of pride in Steve's voice had not gone unnoticed. They were all ten or fifteen years younger than Steve, mostly unemployed, and mostly wearing fashionable, but worn, clothes. Some of them were already dreamy and eloquent on cider and cannabis, but they were boys and lost, and my heart went out to them.

This was the first of many summer nights we would sit together talking on the beach. They talked about life...and death. They shared dreams and experiences, their hopes and fears. I realized that they were quite ordinary youngsters, who, like Steve, somewhere along the line had missed out on a love that accepted them as unique. So they had created their own security, made choices, and then been trapped in their mistakes. They smoked and drank, and I listened and learnt. We laughed a lot.

One night I remember Kev explaining to me, earnestly, all about his trade of bricklaying. He taught me how to build a wall properly. I still treasure that time. Jobless then, Kev`s personality was deep in street culture, drink, and drugs, but he had a huge heart and a spiritual capacity that had survived the muddle life had dealt him. Like the others, he always treated me with the utmost courtesy and respect. This puzzled me, I didn't smoke and I didn't drink much; I just listened. After the inevitable competitions about who could get to the nearest bar and back again unchallenged, high ('stoned') on cannabis, these youngsters would sit, quietly insensible. Kev and I would often watch the sun, a sizzling orange ball, slip blazing past Brighton pier, and sink into the sea, as the sky flamed many colours. Kev would haul himself almost reverently to his feet to watch, swaying slightly on the stones. Then he'd drop down next to me, smiling.

" 'Aint' that bloody marvellous?" he'd say in an awed whisper. I've never forgotten him. I often wonder if he is alive now.

I was always aware that Steve had been bound over into my care by the Court, and I knew the real risk of us getting home from these nights without any sort of incident. Steve's worries were lifted, but mine became heavier. They were always mixed with a terrible sadness. I remember Steve standing on the water's edge one night in the dark, shouting at the sea…and probably at God:

"Why can't I feel like this all the time?" The pain in that cry was enormous. There was no one to realize he was ill with depression too, and it never occurred to me. The illegal drugs masked it so effectively. So, very unsteadily, he'd lean on my shoulder as we began our journey, in a strange version of a fireman's lift. He was very heavy. My own senses mildly dulled, I'd haul him along determinedly. Sometimes he was quiet; sometimes he'd make very funny remarks in my ear. And we never fell, we were never stopped, or mugged, or hurt, always making it safely home.

There was no humour the next morning. Steve would lie immobile in bed, black with despair, head throbbing, body craving, and I began to broaden my radius of Chemists for linctus. More than two bottles a week became noticeable to the local Chemist, because each had to be accounted for by a pharmacist. I would still cringe inside when I approached the counter of any chemist.

Now the nights of waiting for Steve to come home were almost more difficult than being with him. At first I would relax in the suddenly peaceful flat, cleaning, or reading, or praying. As the evening ticked on, unease would begin to grip me. It was because I never knew what sort of state he would be in when he arrived, and I did fear for my own safety. I'd learned, to my cost, that someone on cannabis alone, if a piece was 'bad', could be as violent as someone on anything else. No matter what any statistic today might imply. That might be before the alcohol or the effect of any nightly street drugs. I'd learned by now to be wearing my outdoor shoes when he returned, in case I would have to beat a hasty retreat, and to try to keep one eye on a clear path to the door all the time.

Years of drink and drugs, and now still more, meant that Steve's mind was sometimes completely fragmented, and a seeming personality change might occur without the slightest warning. I had no idea that, earlier in his life, a doctor had labelled him 'depressive personality, bordering on psychotic'. An expansive happy mood would occasionally turn dark and become instantly, unreasonably, violent. Once Steve smashed my favourite wedding present; an ornament of two cuddly elephants with intertwined trunks. I glued it back together knowing deep inside that there was something prophetic in the unity being broken. I ignored it. I learned to recognize the danger signals before the rages came...and get out of the way. Most outbursts were without warning, as Steve lashed out at all the people who had hurt him down the years, who weren't there, and that I couldn't see. Overwhelming terror and the need to survive, kept me alert and hyper-vigilant, endlessly wary until the time he slumped senseless into bed. It was through all these times that I experienced the almost physical enwrapping arms of God; God speaking words in my ears, holding me safe in deep silence, 'with me' in the centre of the frightening chaos. The day after such an outburst Steve would be panic-stricken. He would be sad, and deeply worried that he had hurt me in some way that he could not remember. I would often come from the kitchen in response to a call from the bedroom, early in the morning.

"Piggie…are you all right?"

"Just about."

"Oh no…What did I do? I can't remember a thing." Sometimes I would have to tell him what had happened, or he'd notice a bruise.

"That's me isn't it? I did that. I'm a bad man. I am so sorry." And then he'd be quiet for a long time.

Yet we grew closer as we tolerated each other's shortcomings, large and small. I began to stop my `spiritual` talk, and tried to put it into action more. I tried to learn to cook. I made an effort not to nag, and to go out with him with more good grace. He started spending more time with me at home, and buying me Mars bars and magazines as a 'surprise'. As we began to trust each other more, I learned about lovemaking, too, although fear was always a predictable third party. But the tender moments increased, and one morning a smiling Steve got up, made our bed, and disappeared mysteriously into the kitchen. A man with a purpose.

"What are you up to?"

"Go away, Piggie..." He emerged later from the kitchen with two neatly packed piles of sandwiches, a thermos of tea, and some fruit. All this he put carefully in a carrier bag, as I watched, puzzled.

"We're going out today. I'm taking my Piggie out, it's a surprise! Come on..."

So we walked into Brighton with me badgering him all the way, and jumping up and down at his side like a small child. It was the Pier, of course.

"It's your favourite place, isn't it? I've been saving some money up for today.

Good Dragon..." He was all `claws` and `smiling` dragon teeth. So we spent the day, physical and mental pain conquered; enjoying the freedom of the sea, the deck chairs, dodgems and gift stalls. We ate toffee apples and wrote a postcard to my parents. Steve only had a couple of drinks in the bar at the end of the pier, (and one bottle of linctus), and then we walked home, holding hands. It was a good day. A celebration day. And it still sparkles in my mind as a glimpse of hope. A hope of the way all was intended to be, and of the 'foolishness' of God in bringing us together.

"And then one day
(And I still don't know how it happened) the sea came without
warning, without welcome even…."
(Carol Bullock – Chile '95)

Chapter 13

As the trust between us grew, so did the intimacy, and my mind often wandered on to a brighter future when God's promise of further healing would be fulfilled, for myself as well as Steve. One very big blow for me was the fact that Steve couldn't face the prospect of becoming a father...again. His first son from his previous marriage had died soon after birth. The other, Lee, he never saw, being in the custody of his ex-wife. He was simply unable to contemplate the possibility of more loss. Now, I have an insight into his thinking; then, I was devastated, and remember sobbing for hours after we had discussed the matter. How grateful I am now that there was no child. Instead, we seemed to revel in the childishness in ourselves which somehow capered and slid under and around our circumstances, healing and releasing pain in unforeseen ways. One of the most amazing for me was meeting a certain football thug. On this particular afternoon, Steve had trailed back from the local pub, and sat in a dazed sort of way on our sofa. My 'red alert' lights began to flicker, as I noticed his pin-point pupils and slow movements. We chatted awhile, and then suddenly he slipped easily into an accurate flat London accent. He was a good actor. It was the voice of the lad on the football terraces. He was going to 'do everyone in', a can of beer in one hand, the other waving his team 'footie' scarf. Charmed, in spite of possible physical danger, I stood on dramatic ground that I understood well. Rising to the challenge of improvisation, I posed as a new acquaintance and began to talk to the lad, drawing him out. Steve warmed to the game with enthusiasm. For over an hour he created a character who was mesmerising. No inflection of personality was overlooked. I heard about his tough home life, football terrace fights, how no-one 'loved' him, but he 'didn't care'. He simply beat them up instead. We talked about his 'mates', drink, women, and his apparent joy in destruction. All in the same monotone of badly formed words and confused thoughts. Deep within, a part of me registered that Steve's own pain, rejection, and confusion were being voiced, released, perhaps partially defused, and I knew, faintly, that I was handling dynamite. Yet God's grace prevailed.

After a long time, Steve made as if to stop.

"Forgive me," I said, "do you know, I never even asked your name."

"Hooligan", the 'lad' said dully, and gave me a completely vacant smile.

Creativity often motivated us. One afternoon was spent drawing, in a sudden discovery of repressed talent and joy. Steve produced endless cartoon pictures of a dragon (himself), and a small pig, (me). The pig had very long eyelashes. I was outraged and very amused that each picture put the pig in impossible situations of great danger: the dragon in control. In one, she hung in a basket over a cliff edge, while he hovered with a pair of shears, smiling horribly, at the top of the cliff. I found it very funny. I felt that this thinly suppressed annoyance at my very presence sometimes was being well expressed. Now, I would rather not think much deeper about the possible stronger implications of repressed rage and anger. How well protected God kept me. The drawing I related to most was one that Steve was almost embarrassed about. It was very carefully detailed, and to me it expressed the longing of the child in Steve which called to the longing child in me. He had drawn a small cottage with a neat garden and gate. It was fenced all the way round. In the garden were trees, a pond, and many flowers. Patterned curtains hung at the windows of the cottage, and smoke came out of the chimney. In the middle of the garden stood a smiling dragon...and a small pig. They were holding hands.

We needed the understanding that met in our play. The destructive forces of alcohol and drugs tightened their grip round our lives, afresh. One night someone slipped a barbiturate cocktail into Steve's drink in the pub. A stranger returned to the flat, and held me backwards over the banisters, for what felt like minutes. I heard myself begging him over and over again not to hurt me. Perhaps disgust at my terror, or sudden realization, made him release me; but I prefer to believe an angel intervened. It was the bitter taste in Steve's mouth next day that made him recognize barbiturates, and I had a hard job preventing him from finding the man he knew to be responsible, and beating him to a pulp.

Another time Steve returned from the local pub high on LSD and did not recognize me at all. It was only the strange name 'Pigmeat' that penetrated the insanity, changing unreasonable boiling fury into a smile and a calmer attitude. Then Steve sat up all night simply trying to hang on to his reason. He had often done this in his past. Somehow he hadn't been able to resist trying the drug he so much feared, once again. He had good reason to fear it. One of his old friends now lived in a mental hospital on a continuous 'trip'.

I lived on the edge of fear. More than once now I had to get Steve to hospital quickly for the all-important injection that would either ease withdrawal symptoms, or simply calm him down. We always seemed to arrive in Casualty at about two o'clock in the morning, and wait for a long time before anyone was 'available'. Frequently an exhausted young houseman would consider Steve with thinly disguised disdain.

"I'm not sure he needs an injection. I really don't want to give him one." Once Steve was snarling and raging, shaking and moaning in a nearby cubicle, endless street drugs now wearing off...and I was desperate.

"He's a registered addict."

"Possibly," said this particular doctor, "but it is abuse of drugs." My weary mind began to explode.

"Has it ever occurred to you 'why'? Have you ever thought of what is behind all this?" I shouted. "He is a human being...and he's in pain!" The doctor just shrugged, unmoved. He was plainly disgusted.

One night the combination of innumerable drugs and alcohol turned Steve into an angry maniac, obsessed with his past. Hospital staff put him in a room with just a mattress propped against the wall, and he punched that endlessly for a long time, screaming abuse at his step-father whom he had hated. I was so tired I sat on the floor in the Children's Play Area in Casualty, hugging an enormous teddy bear, and weeping uncontrollably.

"Are you all right?" asked a pretty nurse, as she passed. But she didn't wait for an answer, and I would have given the earth to share with someone, or be held tight. At length I heard Steve shouting,

"Where's my wife? I want my wife!"....and I was directed towards the mattress room. Trembling, I wondered why no-one was going to come with me. God was my only shield. It was a long walk over the harshly lit linoleum floor. What would he do to me when I appeared? All he did do was look at me wearily, like a little boy.

"Let's go home, Piggie, shall we?"

I was in the middle of ironing a pair of jeans one night, when Jessica phoned with some startling news.

"You'll never guess what?" she said dryly, "you and Steve have been thrown out of the Community." It all seemed rather irrelevant.

It appeared that most of the Community members struggling at the now failing Bingo Hall Centre in Brighton had been invited to return to the foundation Community headed by the minister I trusted. Yet their return rested on a basic framework of Scriptural principles. These required strict obedience to the Leadership of the Community, for in the wake of a string of crimes and suicides, the Leadership were taking action. The disaster of the people who were 'too dirty' and had been 'returned to the mud' was becoming apparent. But no such invitation even found its way to us.

Perhaps our 'rebellion' no longer made us suitable Community material...

No-one contacted Steve or me ever again.

At the time, all this hardly made an impression with me. It was simply a fleeting cloud across the sky, as I battled to survive each day. Yet it was only a measure of my sin and selfishness that was demonstrated; and that was what took Jesus to the Cross.

Steve listened angrily as I relayed the phone call from our faithful Jessica.

"I told you the Bingo Hall wouldn't work, but you wouldn't have it. I knew it wouldn't. Just knew..." I felt mortified. My whole life had been tied up in the Community for years in belief and trust. Possibly I had trusted in the wrong thing. Furious, I began rattling on about different peoples' attitudes to us both. Insensitive doctors and spiritual leaders were not far apart in my pained rage.

"It doesn't matter, Piggie," Steve said quietly. Suddenly, he sounded very tired.

"…..And we got on well, the sea and I.
Good neighbours.
Not that we spoke much,
We met in silences respectful, keeping our distances, but looking
our thoughts across a fence of sand."
(Carol Bialock, Chile '75)

Chapter 14

Richard and Bev lived halfway up our road in a roomy basement flat. We'd met them both one evening in the pub at the top of the hill. Richard had been addicted to drugs for years, and his habit had left him weak and dissipated, always in bad health, and quite unable to work, which he strenuously avoided at all costs. Bev worked instead, and although the couple were unmarried, she tended Richard with a devotion that left others puzzled. Steve and Richard welcomed each other with delight, and I drew close to Bev because of the common ground in our partners. In the way and culture of addiction, Steve and Richard used and abused each other in a self-interested sort of way. Alternately egging each other on, and then being critical and self-pitying in the wake of whatever resulted. Privately, I felt superior to Bev, especially when I learned that she often took bus rides along the Sussex coast to different resorts, to buy cough linctus for Richard at the different Chemists. I decided that was dreadful, and those lengths were quite unacceptable. Steve was not nearly so addicted, I told myself. I was actually rather angry with God for allowing us to meet Bev and Richard, and for a number of things I couldn't quite face. Were Christians allowed to be angry? I tried to push my self-righteous feelings down…and they occasionally rebelled. Steve and I would row, and I would stand and shout at him. But God had not left Steve's mind. Bev and Richard heard much about God and Christianity during our friendship. One night Steve stayed up reading Scripture with Richard. Neither of them could sleep anyway because their body metabolism had been so disordered by drink and linctus, but it was the Bible they discussed, not women, guitars, or drugs. Gradually my worst fears were realized. Richard drew a willing Steve further into an addiction to cough linctus, and soon two bottles a day became the minimum. Steve needed to function normally. Without these, he would lie in bed, depressed and lethargic, or haul himself up to sit grumpy and morose in front of the television. He would sometimes not speak at all because he felt so dreadful. But it took me a long while to grasp this, and the constant emotional pain was hard to live with, because above all else I wanted a 'normal' husband. I hated watching whatever it was he was going through. It looked like torture. I hated this daily destruction which he seemed incapable of reversing. I wanted him smiling. I wanted him to share my daily routine. I wanted us to pray together, support each other and perhaps others, with love and a freedom that spoke of Christ. But this quiet, white, depressed man was full of sadness and silence. What could make a dent in this were one or two bottles of linctus and a packet of cigarettes…so each morning I set myself the task of getting them, to lighten the despair.

As our benefit cheques would often simply be consumed by addiction each fortnight, (after vital food stores had been brought), I came to know the places in Brighton where I could sell things for cash. Leaving Steve in bed in the mornings, I'd trot round to these places and sell whatever I'd managed to find. Books, clothes and ornaments all went. My book collection diminished rapidly in my desperation. Once I sold a Bible. It was disappointing; it produced only a third of what I'd expected – a silent parable that increased my gnawing guilt. I even sold my treasured autographed photograph of Jeremy Irons and David Essex in 'Godspell'. It just didn't seem to matter. Now, I was finding it impossible to walk slowly. A combination of anxiety and the need to be back with Steve made me move fast. Sometimes I literally ran from shop to shop.

"You don't give up do you?" remarked a friendly shop owner once. He'd seen me at least twice previously that week. Yet my unrest was not over once I was clutching my precious few pounds. Where would I find a Chemist who would sell me some linctus? Most of the local Pharmacists knew me by now, although I had worked out their duty rotas, and approached a different assistant each visit. Once, not unkindly, I'd been told to go and see a doctor because I had a `problem`. I was often refused a sale. I felt absolutely ashamed. However the sense of victory and hope that came from holding a packet of cigarettes and a bottle of cough mixture made me smile. I felt momentarily calmer…Then my determination would focus on acquiring a second bottle. Sometimes I managed it. I was completely focused on my task because it meant that my husband would be able to function, thus lessening our distress. I believe this basic need for survival was my consuming urge, mingled, somewhere, with compassion and a form of love. Very soon I was doing the very thing that I had despised in Bev. I would catch a bus along the seafront simply to get to a Chemist in a nearby resort.

I had both a sense of delirious freedom as the bus pulled out of Brighton, away from the confining world of our flat and its problems, and a tight, whirring fear about the situation I was in, the seeming impossibility of escaping from it. I can remember one journey vividly. Through the bus window I saw a beautiful field of golden wheat and poppies swaying in the wind, near Rottingdean. For a moment I was caught in wonder, hope, and joy, and rejoiced somewhere I barely remembered. I laughed with the bus driver, enjoying being alive, suddenly free of oppression. Successful that morning, I pocketed one bottle of linctus, and wandered into a beach side café.

That day I had enough money left for a cup of tea and a poached egg, which I consumed with relish. I was alone, safe, and the possibility of a reasonable day stretched ahead of me. Like Bev, I travelled the coast road often in time, snatching the moments of rest and recovery when God gave them. Each day He was graciously repeating the words 'trust' and 'patience' in my head. Each day, over and over again. Words from Isaiah echoed in my mind: "My ways are not your ways...My thoughts not your thoughts..." I felt puzzled and frustrated, yet I knew hope. I was trapped in a sequence of events, seemingly without end or purpose, but my power was in believing that by being still and trusting God within them, He would work out whatever His purposes were for Steve and me.

I used to visit my parents alone. Steve's touchiness and rejection always set off arguments. My parents were a little fearful of him, not understanding his mood changes at all. His feelings of self-condemnation and unworthiness from the past soon settled on them, and he had become convinced he was unwelcome in their home. For their part they had struggled bravely with the explosions, but were now quite relieved when I arrived to see them alone. We would never invite them to Brighton because travel was difficult now that they were becoming older, and we had nowhere, settled, of our own to live. The flat was let only short-term…I preferred too, to keep my parents in ignorance of as many of our problems as I could. My mother was losing her sight, and my ageing father was finding the new role of Carer quite hard. So we all kept in touch weekly, by phone, but inevitably the weekend would come when I needed to travel home.

Once I went because my father explained that, very soon, my mother would be quite blind. But before I left Brighton there were preparations to be made. On this occasion Steve made an appointment to see a doctor about Irritable Bowel Syndrome, an illness he'd suffered from before. He gave a false identity, and submitted to an embarrassing internal examination, so that the doctor would prescribe the required codeine phosphate tablets. This bottle would last him one weekend. Then I washed and ironed his jeans and T-shirts ready for pub visits, and stocked up the larder.

My times away were always carefully planned to coincide with our benefit cheques, Steve being on Invalidity Benefit as a registered drug addict. This particular visit, a quieter Steve bought me some magazines and a Mars bar for the train journey, and we sat unusually close to each other in the pub and at the flat, the day before I left. That morning I got up silently and dressed with a slightly apprehensive heart. Once or twice before, he had asked me to stay with him as he felt ill. This time he didn't open his eyes, but gave me a hug as I bent over the bed.

"Give them my love. Behave yourself, Pigmeat…"

I knew it was difficult for him to let me go, so I was cheerful back, emphasizing my return. Over a year ago he had been worried that I would not return to him. Now he must have been sure. I was torn between two needs, and he must have recognized my dilemma.

It was the last time I saw my mother, for she died some months after my visit, and I was so glad to have spent time with her. We encouraged each other, sharing old jokes and stories, and I found her courage in the face of blindness astonishing. She called God 'the Governor' and was convinced that He was in control of all that was happening. It was quite an emotional moment when we parted, she waving gamely, although she could not see me at all. I found it very difficult walking away from her, down the road, but there seemed a strong gentle force pulling me back to Brighton. I knew God wanted me there. On previous trips I had wondered in an agony of indecision whether I should leave Steve. I dreaded the return journey to pain, and hurt, and danger. This time was different.

A few hours later, very weary in mind and body, I opened our flat door, and made for the lounge. To my surprise the room looked quite tidy. There were no overflowing ash trays, coffee cups, or clothes strewn everywhere, as was usual. Suddenly, my eye caught something perched on the top of the television. A small cuddly toy in the shape of a miserable spaniel puppy was looking at me dolefully. Steve appeared from the bedroom.

"I thought you'd like him...he sort of leapt at me as I wandered round a shop...

He's called 'Happy'" I smiled, stroking the puppy delightedly. Steve seemed pleased, and as I glanced up, I saw that he was smiling broadly.

"He gives power to the faint, and to him who has no might, He increases strength."
(Isaiah 40 v 29 RSV)

Chapter 15

When fit enough, Steve could often be found wandering round the back street guitar shops in Brighton. He would examine different models with an appreciative, but sometimes critical eye. His memories of his days in a band, and his love of rock music would often surface in pub discussions. He had a vast knowledge of music history over the years, yet always returned with deep joy to the great guitarists, classical and rock. The lead guitarist of the music group 'Dire Straits' had been a personal friend in his early days of learning, and had once commented on his style and speed with a guitar. He will never know the jewel he gave a young lad. Now, music was a large chunk of Steve's life. He would often save for weeks to buy a particular music tape, and the flat was generally shuddering to the sound of plaintive guitar, or quality rock singers.

It wasn't long before he had managed to acquire a reasonable acoustic guitar. (From where was a question better not asked), and on his better days he would often sit cross-legged playing in the Brighton 'Lanes'. He would wait, in the network of tiny streets, to secure the best `pitch` from other buskers, and soon he built up quite a following with the tourists and shoppers.

His natural gift and fast inventive style drew appreciative comments, and several offers of night work in high class restaurants in the town. But he never followed them up. He had not the patience or commitment; but he was content to earn money for us when things became harder.

One morning we had literally nothing in the larder, but we did have two bottles of linctus, so Steve was able to get to his Lanes pitch early in the day, and there he stayed. When he returned to the flat in the evening he was carrying a mysterious white plastic bag. It was our supper: fish fingers, peas, potatoes…bottles of brown ale, and a Mars bar for me. He beamed from ear to ear as he prepared our meal, and it tasted like a royal feast.

Pride in Steve was one thing, but my own was a different kettle of fish, as the saying goes. Although we became good at spinning out Benefit Cheque money, the days before the next cheque could be quite grim. I found I missed the small things the most: a magazine, a favourite eye shadow, or perhaps even a luxury pot of honey. For I had no money. Steve held the purse strings because I knew that money was his means of security, even survival, in his emotional life. I didn't have to have money in my pocket to feel safe in this way, to feel in control. Now I lived with the feeling of powerlessness. I knew my existence rested in God's hands. He was in control, so that powerlessness was my friend. I was also quite proud. Once I scribbled an `imaginary shopping list` on a piece of paper. Steve found this screwed up in the waste paper bin. The next time he went out with some money, he came back laden. There was a pot of honey, some magazines, and a bag of apples for me…treasure indeed. He looked shamefaced.

"I'm so sorry I've been so selfish, Piggie. Me spending all I do on drink when you needed things…I just never thought."

Every time we did our fortnightly shopping from then onwards, he would make me choose some small personal things for myself, and give me as much money as was possible. He never forgot. Often in the midst of chaos, I would find Mars bars or sweets on my pillow. They were the tastiest things I will ever eat.

One afternoon the flat seemed to be invaded by dishevelled teenage boys, who sat and talked to Steve with obvious respect. They draped themselves round the lounge and listened to music, being polite and quiet to me. As I made the usual mugs of coffee, I learned that they were all waiting for the right moment to visit another flat in the town, that of a drug dealer. All of them had decided to try LSD.

"How wise is that?" I asked one worriedly, handing him his coffee. I felt like his mother.

"Won't know till I try," he grinned, completely unrepentant. I cornered my husband.

"What are you going to do?" I hissed, "can't you stop them?"

"They won't listen," he said calmly, "I can't stop them." I was stricken.

"But what are you going to do?" I felt, passionately, that it was his responsibility.

"I'm going to stay with them. Someone has to." I retreated in horror, my mind scrambling round with terrifying thoughts.

"I won't be taking any, Pigmeat," Steve said behind me, as if reading my mind, "I've had quite enough of the stuff, thank you very much! Don't worry."

It was difficult not to worry. The little band trooped off and returned late in the evening like a pack of small zombies. They lay down or curled themselves round the lounge, becoming lost in music and hallucination. All night I lay tense in bed, alone, praying. I slept only fitfully. I crept into the room in the early morning. There were only two boys left. One was propped in a corner watching a plant pot with distracted eyes. The other lay full length on the sofa. Steve was collapsed comfortably in an armchair, keeping an eye on the boy in the corner. He looked up and smiled at me as I came in.

"Hello Piggie!…I'd love some coffee…"

"Are you…all right?" I asked nervously.

"I'm fine." he said easily. He sounded normal. "But it's been quite a night." He grinned at the boy in the corner, in an almost paternal sort of way.

"He tried to fly from the window. He'll be all right, though."

Steve certainly had the ability to meet people and tune in to their need, especially if they were struggling to survive, and he always responded with the same force and promptness. After drinking sessions, he brought back to the different places we lived in Brighton many different characters who mirrored his own sadness and loneliness, or who had suffered great loss or hardship in their lives.When the drink ran out coffee and talk, and listening ears were all we had. I often grew very weary of hour upon hour of people who did not want to go home, or who had nowhere to call home. I had very little patience, and felt trapped and isolated. Sometimes I stopped smiling and serving coffee, and simply went to bed, emotionally exhausted.

Yet Steve craved company, scheming, striving, to build for himself some sort of basis of self worth, even whilst still chasing destruction. He managed somehow to mingle with this the truth of the gospel, and a genuine compassion for others. We were in a queue in a Wimpy Bar in Brighton one night, when he saw a tramp being turned away because he did not have enough money to pay for a single leg of chicken. Everyone watched in silence. Steve pushed to the front of the queue, and slammed some money down on the Formica counter.

"You give him what he wants," he told the alarmed girl serving. She obeyed very quickly.

"There you are, mate." Steve handed the man the food in a rough, kindly way. The man was overcome.

"Thank you so much, son. Thank you so much. You're the first person that's spoken to me today…"

Before we left, we went over to his corner table, and shook him by the hand a long time. I thought my heart would burst.

We still saw Richard and Bev from time to time, and they sometimes turned up with friends to play cards or smoke dope. Yet sometimes Steve seemed to grow weary with this lifestyle himself. I remember a winter evening he spent trying to fix some Christmas tree lights on a small Christmas tree we'd placed near our lounge window. A dazed Richard kept calling him to come and join in the card game. Eventually, without turning round, Steve replied tiredly,

"Look, I'm busy, man. I want to fix these lights. My wife likes Christmas tree lights."

I was beginning to feel more like a wife. I knew I was appreciated, although I could never quite come to terms with the idea that I might be loved, or desired. I watched women in pubs eyeing Steve. I saw their faces change almost imperceptibly as I was introduced, and I knew, too, that Bev herself had tried to seduce Steve at their flat once, when they were alone.

"And….?" I'd demanded icily.

"I didn't." Steve said shortly. "She's quite attractive…" Then he grinned as I realized he was teasing me. He still had a string of very unattractive names for women in general, and was most dismissive of them. He particularly detested his mother.

"But I'm a woman!" I'd wail in frustration.

"You're different," he'd say. And that was that.

"Thy right hand supported me and Thy help made me great. Thou didst give a wide place for my steps under me and my feet did not slip." (Psalm 18 v 35,36 RSV)

"One doesn't discover new lands without consenting to lose sight of the shore for a very long time." (Andre Gide)

Chapter 16

Right in the middle of the summer that year, the landlord of our flat telephoned us to tell us we would have to look for a new home, as he wanted to sell his property. I thought I felt the chill come over Steve's heart, and the next weeks were again badly chaotic with drink and drugs.

We both tried to keep anxiety at bay. I prayed and listened and waited. I can remember our walking along the sea front one blazing hot day, Steve drunk, weaving in and out of the holiday makers, and carrying a huge flagon of white wine to drink on the beach. The lost children were on the move again. Earlier, I had spotted an advert in the local paper and suddenly felt bold to phone the landlord of a large house in another area of Brighton. He gave us a time to visit him. Against all the odds, he accepted us as the new tenants of a smart newly decorated bed-sit in his house. I reflected that one of the Hebrew names for God is 'Provider'.

Our bed-sit room was medium sized, with a glass door that led to a long galley kitchen, and a small toilet and shower. The room had French windows with wooden shutters that we could shut at night, for our home overlooked a very busy, noisy main street. Opposite stood a huge red brick church, where pigeons were roosting obsessively on the roof. A few doors away, round the corner, was our new local pub.Life resumed in this new area, much the same as it had done before. Time went on with a new procession of visiting characters that had all the same problems. Yet I felt positive about being in a new place, the influence of Richard and Bev had gone, and there was the possibility that God would provide new positive relationships through which to work for our good. Carol and Ben lived together in the bed-sit across the corridor from us. They were seemingly sensible, drug free, and friendly, and they appeared to accept Steve and me straight away in a non-judgmental sort of way. We all shared meals together in the café in the High Street, and I was able to push further and further down inside, my pain about Steve's addiction to cough linctus. Winter began, Christmas came and went.

I was sitting reading quietly one afternoon in February when I heard Steve's key in the lock. He came into the room looking distracted, and the familiar fear motor began in me instantly.

"What's the matter?" I demanded, as he sat down next to me looking very strange.

"It's Lee," he said, "he's dead." The shock of horror hit me from head to foot. I burst into tears.

"Why are you crying?" Steve asked, looking at me in a dazed sort of way.

"Because I'm sad for you." I snuffled. It was not entirely true. I was terrified what madness the death of his small son would evoke, as Steve idolized him. Each time he'd taken his name or life as 'proof' of a truth he was speaking, I'd felt very uneasy. I couldn't have known what was to happen, but I'd felt odd each time. This day Steve had responded to an inner prompting and phoned his friend in the North, charged with keeping an eye on Lee, and his mother. Steve learned that on Christmas Eve his son, now eleven, had been walking with a friend along a narrow lane near a country Social Club. A car had come fast round the bend, driven by a drunken driver, and both boys had been killed outright. Steve's dream of his son coming to find him was over. He had gone to the nearest doctor and asked for an injection of Valium, which accounted for his disconnected state, and which revealed to me even more of the workings of the mind of an addict; no opportunity was missed. I had no idea what would happen when the drug wore off, but I thought I could make some very intelligent guesses.

I was wrong. Mainly I listened to Steve as he told me all about Lee for days, then I made sure he got to bed. He slept a lot. I prayed a lot. The most difficult job I had was convincing him that going back up North, tracing and killing the driver of the car, was not the best idea. And after the rage and grief came the despair. Steve would simply lie quietly in bed for days. But a very strange thing had happened.

The morning after the tragic news, I'd gone shopping, and I'd felt God speaking to me about Lee. The phrase that kept filling my head was, "...for his protection..." Before I could say a word when I got back to our bed sit, Steve said,

"It's all right, Piggie. It's all right. I know this sounds daft, but God's just told me."

"I know," I said, and told him about the words. We considered together. Steve wondered if Lee had been in physical danger from his step-father (as Steve had been when younger), but now, looking back, I believe God was protecting him from a life as broken and dangerous as his Dad's. Perhaps a severe mercy, a higher way than ours. The experience of hearing God so clearly increased my faith and humbled us both. We felt He was truly involved in our lives. Steve said that perhaps God understood because His own Son had been killed, too.

It was a little while after this that I suddenly began to battle with alarming symptoms of depression, my oldest enemy. I would feel too frightened to get up, or go outside the room, and my head began to feel very peculiar indeed. I didn't recognize my feelings at first (as is often the way), and then one morning a strange name simply dropped into my mind, seemingly from no-where. It was then I remembered it was the name of an anti-depressant tablet that I had found helpful years previously.

I went to the Doctor's, where I suddenly couldn't speak for tears. The Receptionist was a kindly lady, who sat me down and gave me a cup of tea, before our Doctor prescribed me exactly the tablets of the past. The relief was enormous. Gradually I began to feel more normal; the tablets were doing their work. At a guess, my furious anger with Steve and the world had simply compressed itself into clinical depression, because I couldn't or wouldn't release it. I feared the consequences too much. My fear was enormous. I now became quieter.

"You don't shout at me so much, Piggie," Steve commented thoughtfully. I wonder, now if this was good....or not.

Steve was beginning to become slightly weaker physically. A shopping trip, returning carrying a bag heavy with tins, would leave him sitting exhausted for a while afterwards. Yet his sense of the ridiculous was quite undimmed. Once he came from the kitchen after storing the food from such a trip, and remarked to me,

"Arnie is sitting by the fridge again." Arnie was a small, tenacious, imaginary dragon who was completely obsessed with food. He would appear whenever we had a full larder, and wait hopefully. I knew exactly what he looked like. When we ate sausages and bacon we had to shut him in the kitchen, or shoo him away.

"Is he? I responded, "Well, he's got no chance..."

"I know," Steve said seriously, "I told him that, but it's the chicken. He knows it's in the fridge."

One Brighton character who spent much time with us was a young lad called Dave. Dave was interested in learning to play the guitar. He was open and likeable, streetwise and loyal, and he had no home of his own. We spent hours together over cider, coffee and cigarettes, and a strong relationship grew. He came to regard our Bed-Sit as a place of safety, which was sometimes difficult when Steve was too deep in drug withdrawal symptoms to want to see anyone at all. I would often have to explain to Dave, and ask him to come back another time. One such time was three weeks after Lee's death, when snow was beginning to fall gently outside our shutters.

Steve groaned when our door bell rang. He had not got up that morning, unable to face the day. I felt so distracted by our circumstances that I couldn't concentrate on being civil either. I didn't answer the door. A couple of hours later, Steve ran out of cigarettes. I knew that at least these helped to ease the tension of the pain of muscle cramps, and heard myself offer to go and buy him some. On our doorstep, in the snow, sat Dave. I nearly tripped over him as I went out. He got up stiffly, looking worried.

"Jenny, your mother's been taken ill. She's had a heart attack, and she's in hospital. I was at Jed's when a call came…" Unreality walloped me round the face; it must be a mistake. We had given our friend Jed's number to my parents for emergencies, and this sounded like one. Dave had sat for over an hour in the snow to be sure of catching me. He thought we were out.

So began the strange terrible sequence of events and emotions that are bereavement, all over again. My mother died that night. Yet within the pain, I had a strange certainty that she had simply gone home to her `Governor's` house. Steve and I both struggled to support my father at his flat for the next week or so, and then trailed miserably back to the Brighton Bed-Sit. We were both completely emotionally exhausted. For Steve, the funeral had touched the raw nerve of the death of his son, and for me there was a hole in my life that would never be filled again. Now, grief, anger, and pain often had us snarling and shouting at each other. It seemed to go on a long time. I felt more alone that I ever had done before, and I missed my mother's warm loving voice over the telephone more than I could say. She always made me feel that I wanted to run into her arms. But now there were no arms, except those of God. He never let me go.

After a particularly furious row with Steve, one night, I wandered round the streets in the dark, sobbing. I ended up sitting on some stairs in a nearby block of flats. I had no idea what I was going to do, or where else to go. I wasn't even sure who I was, in the first place. As I sat and cried, I suddenly became aware of some small children watching me in an awed sympathetic sort of way. Soon most of them drifted away. All but one small girl who looked around eight. She eventually stepped across the landing and looked up at me.

"What's the matter?" she asked directly.

"Well," I said with difficulty," my mum has just died...and I've had a row with my husband, and I don't know what to do..." She watched me seriously as I wept.

"My name's Laura."

"Hello, Laura. My name's Jenny." I blew my nose, and sat gulping.

"I live here. My mum and dad are always shouting at each other. Where do you live?`"

"Oh...around." I said vaguely. She scrambled up and sat on the stair below me looking up thoughtfully.

"Do you think you had better go home, because your husband will be worried about you?" It was clear adult wisdom.

"I don't think so..." I sobbed.

"He will," she said. Light began to filter into my head. The concrete stair suddenly felt very hard. I smiled at her.

"Yes, Laura. You're absolutely right. Thank you." I got up slowly.

"Goodbye," said the little girl. I walked back to our bed-sit with a heavy heart. As I entered the hall of the house, I met Carol and Steve just coming down the stairs. Relief spread all over their faces.

"Where have you been? We were just coming to find you." I couldn't speak.

"I've just fed your dinner to the dog..." Steve joked, in an attempt to break my mood.

"We haven't got a dog..." I said stupidly.

"Come on Piggie...I'll make you some more supper. I was worried..."

He fussed over me with a sort of guilty tenderness, concerned too, that Carol wouldn't think the row had been his fault. With great wisdom she made sure that I could cope, before disappearing firmly back into her room opposite. Steve alternated between grumbling and affection, but he held me very close that night. We became gentler with each other after that, both very aware that the other was in pain. I sensed God, too, in the change of attitude. He was concentrating upon taking one day at a time.

"My God will provide all you need from His riches in Christ Jesus."
(2 Corinthians 8 v 8 RSV)

"To the outcast on her knees,
You're the God who really sees." (El Shaddai – Celtic Worship)

Chapter 17

Although our financial situation became easier after the death of my mother, this proved to be a mixed blessing. Once again I had to come to terms with my husband's addiction and obsession with money. Intent on security, Steve seemed almost hungry for our share of my mother's will. I found this very painful indeed, especially as I knew that more money undoubtedly meant more drugs and drink. I had managed to stall my parents` previous offers of financial help many times, but now I was powerless against the inevitable tide of destruction that threatened to overwhelm me, via wealth. I slid back towards depression, and my tablets were increased.

Now Steve could indulge himself, a little like Toad of Toad Hall in 'Wind in the Willows', in whatever hobby took his fancy. These crazes, like his absorption in music, seemed a defence against the real world. They validated his own worth in his world. At the start of our time in our High Street bed-sit, the interest was pot plants. The room resembled a greenhouse. Then Steve moved on, to a collection of unusual rings, and then, knives. I was sent to various shops in Brighton to acquire these things, if withdrawal symptoms prevented him getting out of bed.

The knives were probably his most dangerous collection. I once had one whizz past my ear in the middle of a heated argument. Once he managed to set up a target shooting range, with the bull's-eye in the kitchen, which he could shoot at quite comfortably from the sofa in the lounge. The pellets from the target shooting rifle often smashed the glass in the small kitchen window, despite the fact that he was an excellent shot. I don't remember now how we explained the noise and broken panes to our Landlord, but our drinking friends were enchanted.

Through the crazes, I was intent on supporting and inspiring Steve, also simply trying to keep the peace. I battled with my own indignation and fright. I knew I was often in very real physical danger, yet God's protection prevailed. I detested being trapped in this small space, often listening endlessly to loud music. I was often quite angry and wanted to run away. I sometimes crept out early in the morning for some quiet time on my own, becoming good at turning the door handle completely noiselessly.

My thinking then was that anything that occupied and engrossed Steve took his mind off drink and drugs. I seemed to be there to enable, and keep an eye on safety and practicality. It was not unlike containing a damaged toddler in the best possible way, mixed with the fear of being unable to do it successfully.

The latest interest was a new video recorder on which were all manner of films, of every quality imaginable.

The hardest films for me were the sudden influx of horror and war films shot in America about the Vietnam war. Hours were consumed sitting before the blood, gore and violence. These films were gruesome and realistic, and I hated them. As the room was so small there was nowhere to be without seeing or hearing them in some way. Steve believed his real father had been a member of the SAS, and was completely fascinated by combat techniques and warfare. There may well have been truth in his conclusion from his father's guarded stories when they met, and I could see this was a way of him feeling closer to the man who had died years previously. But the badly made videos sickened me.One day, consumed with revulsion, I went for a walk, and ended up sitting on the low wall in front of a local Evangelical church. I wondered what God would think of the whole situation....As if on cue, a concerned woman seemed to appear from nowhere. I poured out my problem of being endlessly faced with terrible images that I couldn't escape, when it was my husband's turn to choose a film. This lady was very firm and kind, and said exactly what I needed to hear.

"God knows the situation. He knows exactly how you feel. He understands you."

Some days later, as I sat dully before the TV screen with Steve, while an impossible 'Technicolor' adventure rambled on, some words interrupted my despair. They formed strongly in my head.

"Do you think that your way is hidden from Me? I have not forgotten you." And then I knew the truth of them, and was comforted.

God knew, too, about the increasing dangers to Steve that extra money was bringing. One lunchtime, Steve brought a tall man with a crew cut back to our room. As the man came through the door the word 'snake' dropped into my mind. A little later he went to 'make a phone call', after which he and Steve set out for the pub. Hours later the bed-sit door crashed open and a euphoric Steve burst in. He lifted me straight into his arms, and whirled me round, as his new friend watched. Then he sat down suddenly on the sofa, looking odd. As I watched Steve began to breathe heavily, turning quite white.

"What's the matter?" I yelled. I turned to the man. "What's the matter with him? Call an ambulance...quick!"

"NO," said the man instantly, edging towards the door. Steve's lips began to turn blue.

"Please...help me!" I screamed. The man stopped. He seemed to decide something. He began to pull Steve up.

"Get him on his feet...black coffee..." We hauled the leaden body upright, and the man dragged Steve round the room until he took his own tottering steps, and began to breathe properly. Then I tried to get scalding coffee through his clenched teeth. Some trickled down his chin. It seemed an age before he began to choke on it, the colour flooding back into his face. Only then I turned round to the man, but he had gone. The 'snake' had been a heroin dealer.

One night Steve had only been gone to the local pub for about an hour when there was a knock on the bed-sit door. When I opened the door there was no-one there, and I was just about to close it again, with a sigh of exasperation, when I noticed something sitting at my feet. It was a soft toy leopard cub, the size of a small puppy. I swept him into my arms and cried all over him.

He was very realistically made, and had a sweet, wise expression. I sat with him on my lap all evening until I heard Steve returning.

"Who's that then?" he asked, coming into the room. He sounded puzzled.

"This is Sam," I said, "He's come to live with us. He arrived this evening."

"Did he indeed? Well, I hope he doesn't like chicken. And you'd better keep him out of Arnie`s way. He'll be furious."

Steve had seen Sam being sold for charity in the pub, and thought I would like him. But from then on Sam became our trusted companion, often listening with great patience to both of us, when we thought the other was out of earshot.One night a female visitor demanded that Sam should go home with her, Steve and I shouted

"NO!" at exactly the same moment. She was astonished. Sam had come to stay.

Our doctor was obviously `sympathetic` to our problems, having prescribed the right tablets to help me, and she was remarkably tolerant of Steve's moods and rages. She recognized that a registered addict needs chemical support. I think she thought she had the measure of this particular addict, but the reality was that he often emerged from her Surgery with a prescription for slightly more drugs than was actually quite legal.

Steve was a master at eliciting female support. This became apparent to me the day he had a 'grand mal' fit, and crashed through the glass of the kitchen door. He had taken twenty-two pain-killing tablets at once. From then on, I never knew when one of the epileptic-type fits would seize him, and I took to carrying a spoon around to clamp between his teeth. He would suddenly snort and convulse from head to foot, foaming at the mouth. He never remembered anything afterwards, had a terrible headache, and often a cut, swollen tongue where his chattering teeth had caught it.

Apparently there came a point where his brain-wave pattern instantly distorted, a certain amount of one chemical bringing violent reactions. The fits were unpredictable, which was almost the most frightening thing about them. Only if I knew how many tablets he had taken could I be properly alerted, but this was very difficult. How many waves has the sea? I lived in great tension as we were travelling a lot at the time, visiting my father, and a fit on a crowded train or platform would have presented problems. Steve had already had one, completely unexpectedly, in the local Supermarket, sending tins and packets flying. A gentle, concerned Manager had helped me to pin him to the floor. Frantic, I began to be super-vigilant again, trying to calculate tablets, but an addict is secretive and evasive, so my uncertainty increased.

One morning, months later, his weekly prescription from our doctor was particularly generous, "as it's Christmas." the GP said dryly. A delighted Steve floated through the next few days, whilst I could have cried with rage. Inevitably, when the tablets decreased, Steve went and literally pounded on the Surgery door. There were no further prescriptions forthcoming until the coming week. This felt like a death sentence to Steve, physically, mentally, and emotionally. His body went into complete rebellion, so I returned from the shops later that day to find him lying on the bed-sit floor. There was a note scribbled in blue chalk on an old piece of brown paper, lying nearby. It was all he'd been able to find. Mercifully, time stops me remembering the whole note, but I do remember the words, "I want to die," in shaky capitals. He'd simply taken the remaining tablets, and goodness knows what else. Suddenly anger surfaced, and I shook him furiously. He stirred, managing to tell me to 'go away'. Terrified I beat on his chest with my fists, and then somehow managed to haul him into a sitting position. He opened his eyes with an effort, very slowly.

"I don't want to go on, Piggie, I can't...I haven't got any friends..." There was a pause. "I've got you but...it's not the same...I want to die."

"Well, I don't want you to," I retorted, "If you think you're going to, you've got another thought coming!" There was a faint smile. He tried again.

"That doctor doesn't understand. I hurt...She might as well have killed me..."

This was not the moment to point out that it was up to him to take responsibility for himself. If this was an act it was good. I slipped two cigarettes from a nearby packet into one hand, and lit them both. I didn't smoke, but I did in that moment. We sat silently, propped up against the sofa. Then I talked and talked. He stayed awake. I made some tea, and we sat for hours. Then he crawled into bed and lay there quietly. Most of that night he had painful muscle cramps all over his body. He said it was his own fault and he deserved it. Whilst I knew this was partly true, my anger at the unprofessional doctor was enormous. I felt vindicated some months later to learn that the local drug squad had the practice under investigation.

This was the third time, whilst we were together, that Steve attempted to take his life. Once he swallowed a bottle of bleach, once he tried another overdose. I called the ambulances; faintly seeing a thread of black comedy when one paramedic took a glimpse at Steve's face the second time, and remarked,

"Ere...don't I know 'im'?"

I had no idea, of course, that addicts are extremely high on most 'suicide risk' lists, and only discovered years later, reading some, that Steve had most of the qualifications in his life to date.

"Over this dead loss to society you pour your precious ointment.
Call the bluff and laugh at the fat and clock-faced gravity of our
economy."
(Sydney Carter)

"What is man that You make so much of him and that You set
Your mind upon him. You visit him every morning, and test him
every moment….."
(Job 8 v 17,18 – RSV)

Chapter 18

In the early days after my mother's death we visited my father once a fortnight. He was struggling to cope and both glad and uneasy to see his son-in-law. Their relationship moved forward out of necessity, helped by the fact that they both enjoyed a drink of whiskey. The two men made a tremendous effort to accept each other, mainly for my sake, forgiving and trying to forget former differences. My father's generosity of spirit amazed me, as did his generosity with his possessions. Once a director in a well known auction house, he had been a fine art valuer, and now had gathered tasteful antiques and ornaments with which to furnish his home. Steve had always been fascinated because he loved quality. Yet as his desperation for funds to feed his habit increased, he viewed these expensive things in a different way. Much of his younger life had been involved with crime, and he was still drawn to the possibility of security and pleasure that resulted in financial gain. In the past he'd often persuaded me to ask for some trinket from my father for myself. He would then sell it when we returned to Brighton.

Now, as my father brokenly admitted, material things were meaning less and less to him, a very real pressure loomed. There is a dark side to all human character, and I saw this being honed with the greed of pure lust in Steve. I watched in agony as several valuable ornaments changed hands. But worse was to come. For some time, Steve had been deteriorating physically, and now his stomach was the problem. He began to bring up bile continuously. An X-ray, taken at the time of his arrest previously, had revealed that part of his liver was almost fossilized. Now the pain was sometimes intense. He was obviously struggling and in discomfort.

When he realised there was a problem, my father immediately offered Steve the opportunity to see a Specialist. It was impossible to describe how I felt. I knew, straight away, that Steve would never see one. Of course it did not stop him accepting the cheque, and in subsequent months actually trying to convince me that he was going to consulting rooms in Brighton. Very quietly God's Spirit confirmed the truth in my heart. Eventually, I confronted Steve angrily. He denied it, equally angry, but then broke down and cried. He admitted he had been to the specialist for the first appointment and had been faced with the probability of an operation for a stomach ulcer. Each time since his 'visits' to the specialist had simply been days alone in Brighton. He couldn't understand how I knew, being a master of deception, and no mean actor. I had come to understand him, and could generally tell if a performance was truthful, or even the tiniest bit halting. But it was God, too, who confirmed my suspicions, and pointed quietly to forgiveness. To me this felt completely impossible. Rage, sadness, and disgust battled within me. Somehow, to deceive me was tolerable, but to deceive my unsuspecting father was reprehensible. I found that I did not even like the man who could do this sort of thing. Why had he not died years before he met me, when his heart had stopped for minutes…? The pain was all-consuming, and shook me for days. I came to rest on the fact that I loved Steve. I could not escape that. There was a love within that pulled me towards the only decision I could make. I needed to understand why Steve had attempted this scale of deception, and to ask God to help me work at forgiveness. He had put the love within, and now He must do the same with forgiveness at my request. So that was what I did.

Now Steve became recharged with guilt and shame, and emotions I couldn't hope to plummet, only watch their outworking again with sadness. Flagons of cider all but replaced the cough linctus, and sometimes I had the strength to refuse to go and get him more cider late at night, sometimes not. When he didn't fall into a merciful sleep, the alcohol would often trigger strange behaviour and sudden violence. I could never relax until I heard him fast asleep beside me. The next morning there would be the usual tears of repentance and promises, and I began to get weary. My anti-depressant tablets no longer seemed to be working.

One terrible night I can remember throwing some clothes in a suitcase and fleeing from the flat, as whatever it was Steve had thrown, crashed against the door behind me. I walked down the dark street distractedly, blindly going nowhere. Twenty minutes later I turned into a large modern church with a strangely unlocked door. I sat and wept in a wooden pew, my suitcase beside me. When the storm subsided, I looked up tiredly and the first thing I saw was Jesus on the cross. There was a large crucifix over the elaborate altar. As I stared, I was held, and I realized again that what I was experiencing was very little to what He had experienced, hanging there for me.

A long time later I trailed back home. Steve was asleep. The next morning he remembered nothing at all.

Another time I found myself pacing the pavement down by the sea front muttering angrily, "That's it. I'm leaving.." Blind fury and an indescribable rage had locked my senses into this seemingly irreversible course of action. I thought I would burst. Then gentle words drifted across my mind. Like a breeze.

"That's all right. You're quite free to do that. But I'd like you to stay."

I knew the source of the words, and wept with frustration. I had promised to serve the 'poor and needy', I had dedicated my life to this, years earlier. Now one of the most desperate representatives of these people was again breaking up my life, my mind and my heart. Was this what that dedication had meant? In a Christian bookshop, days earlier, I had picked up a book by Mother Teresa, and read about Christ residing in those she served, in His 'distressing disguise'. Suddenly, a new way of caring and coping opened within me. This enabled me to cope with the pain of abuse in the days that followed, for Steve was often out of control. Caught in self-loathing and fury, I was the nearest thing on which to express his pain. I stayed in this situation with probably the greatest difficulty I had experienced to date. Not out of any sort of heroism or self righteous religiosity, but because I believed the love that God had placed within me would be the victor, and this was what He was asking me to do. I find I believe the same thing today.

"You are a strange and beautiful species. Shall I tell you what I find the most beautiful about you? You are your very best when things are at their very worst."
('Starman' – John Carpenter)

Chapter 19

It was now that Steve began to sell off the numerous guitar accessories he'd been able to buy to provide more cash for his drink and drugs. His moods were constantly swinging between light and dark, with no seeming real cause except of chemical foundation. He spent hours listening to tapes on our new tape deck. This luxury, bought with money inherited from my mother, became his newest obsession. By fine tuning the highly technical controls, he could make the music he so loved sound its very best. The difficulty was that, very often high on drink or drugs, he would not bother to use the expensive earphones. There are music tapes I cannot listen to even now, because of my memories of endless repetitions at damaging volume. Particular songs bring to mind vivid pictures of Steve in a completely altered state. Once, he believed he was Roger Daltry, the lead singer of the band the `Who`, and he ran on the spot for hours, as Daltry used to do while performing. The same day he had thrown a pub acquaintance of ours down the stairs after an imaginary insult. Rushing to our room, Carol had realized something I'd missed: Steve was on heroin.

She and Ben promptly locked up their bed-sit opposite and quietly disappeared for a time. Ben had been called upon to mend a kicked-in door once previously, after a drug session.He had no intention of being available again. Feeling betrayed and deserted myself, I went for a trembling walk, leaving the room throbbing with loud sound, Steve still 'running'. I had no idea where he'd got the drug from, just when he'd taken it, or when it would wear off. I suddenly knew a net of evil was closing round us despite my horrified watchfulness, and alert fury. I had even stopped taking my tablets, for they were having no more effect than Smarties.

Now, each day was a roller-coaster of tension and fear. In the force and speed of the clamouring emotions, one small clear voice continually spoke reassurance and safety. God was asking me to keep trusting Him. I actually had no choice. I had very little emotional energy left for anything else.

In between the episodes of chemical madness Steve would be very quiet, almost weary, a subdued state untouched by much stimulation at all. Physically his weakness was increasing. He slept for long periods and did not eat much. He was obviously depressed. These were the times when we would watch more than two videos a day, now quite interesting films, and our evening meal again became a focal point for us both. Steve would sometimes struggle to cook this as a treat for me, being quite unable to manage to eat it himself. He was often violently sick without any reason known to me, and was not sleeping for nights on end. Once, in desperation he went and telephoned a member of the Community who had given him permission to do this, long ago, at our wedding. The man was uncomfortable and said he might be able to see Steve `in the lunch hour` of his Community work. Back at our room Steve sat for a long time silently gazing into space. He looked completely lost. I immediately set out on a cigarette and linctus hunt, full of deep rage and determined compassion.

It was not only Steve's body that was buckling under the onslaught of abuse. His scrambled mind often re-lived past emotional traumas. Sometimes he would write tortured letters to his mother, which he never posted. He was plainly bitter, and furious that she had been unable to support him as he grew up. Equally obviously, he still longed for her love and acceptance. His inability to work at forgiveness crippled his efforts at inner peace. This conflict often worked itself out on me in violent words and actions which he later bitterly regretted. It seemed as if his struggling body kept catapulting him back in time to re-live past hurts and rejections. I simply felt torn apart. I wanted to wipe all the pain away somehow and bring him healing, but I could do nothing except share these days, and pray.

A short walk from our home, there was a butcher's shop which became a place of pilgrimage to us, when money and health permitted. The butcher had won prizes for the excellent sausages he made. Steve's grandmother had taught Steve delicious variations on cooking these favourite delights, and now her grandson put them to good use. I'd sit in gleeful anticipation as glorious smells wafted into our room from the kitchen. I would be banished to the sofa as Steve cooked, and I made the most of trying to sneak theatrically to the stove for a taste before the appointed time.

"Well," Steve would say, stirring the sausages and onions deftly, "my dinner is coming on a treat. I'm really looking forward to this…"

"So am I," I'd say, on cue.

"You?" He'd look surprised, "but you're not getting any. This is mine. Goodness, I'm really hungry…"

"But…but I'm hungry…"

"Well, I'm afraid that's just too bad, really. What a shame. Arnie…! Arnie!" he'd call, "Come on, lad… Dinner's nearly ready!…"

The meal was always delicious. We'd have to lock a disgruntled Arnie in the kitchen, of course, while we ate, and he must have been mortified because there were never any scraps left over for him.

When I prayed now, God always spoke to me about patience and trust. Tiredness melted my protest at the edges. I saw that the bucking horse on the end of the rope was quieter, the rope itself shorter, and I went on clinging to God's promise that He was going to heal my husband. He had never let me down yet.

Our local pub was large and gloomy, notorious for its fights on Friday and Saturday nights, and for its loud unskilful bands. We had come to know the landlady and some of the regular customers, and we would often sit in the same corner of the lounge. One night, as soon as we were seated, I began to feel very uneasy about a man standing at the bar. Deep fear began to flutter within me as Steve brought me my drink and then returned to talk to this man. I knew with absolute certainty he was drug dealer. I also knew that if he offered Steve any drugs, I would simply get up and pour my drink all over his head.

I knew I would actually do it. I was idly wondering what would happen in the ensuing fight, because Steve would hit him for offending me, when Steve himself suddenly came back to our table. He picked up his jacket from the seat beside me.

"We're leaving, Jenny."

"But....I've only just got my drink..." I was shocked.

"Never mind that. Come on" Almost angry, he pulled me up and guided me towards the door. Once outside, he caught my hand and began walking very fast towards home.

"Sorry, my Piggie..." he said.

"What's this all about?" I asked, somewhat breathlessly, trotting at his side. He stared ahead, looking grim.

"That guy at the bar. He's a heroin dealer. I can't resist it. I don't want it, because once I'm on it...I know that's it. This is all getting too heavy for me...too close. I just can't handle it anymore...Piggie...we must leave Brighton."

I knew he was right.

"But He is unchangeable and who can turn Him? What He desires, that He does. For He will complete what He appoints for me."
(Job 23 v 13,14 RSV)

"There is no way anyone can understand what it's like being an addict, unless they've been there."
(Addict - 'Jailbirds' - BBC 1 1999)

Chapter 20

We decided to accept my father's offer of a home with him, at his flat. He had made the offer, cautiously, some time ago, and we had received it with equal caution. Then we had chosen to refuse, but keep in touch daily by phone. Yet now seemed the right moment to accept with gratitude; but all three of us must have had different expectations from the move.

Steve and I left Brighton at eight thirty one morning in a huge removal van sent courtesy of my father's firm. We had very few belongings, and a great deal of relief. I had left the bed-sit as clean and tidy as I could, and written an apologetic letter to the Landlord about the cracked kitchen window, and the cigarette burns on the sofa. It was the end of an era. Steve presented my father with a bottle of his favourite whiskey on our arrival, and I remember sitting on my father's sofa in the large, beautifully furnished lounge feeling mildly shocked at the contrast between that and the surroundings we had just left. `Now,` I thought, `we will be safe at last.` I couldn't have been more wrong.

Instead of one man to keep an eye on, now I was faced with two. They didn't get on particularly well with each other, and they both enjoyed a drink. Now there came the difficulty of adjusting to an elderly widower's set pattern of life, maintaining the peace that brooded between that and the creeping fears of the younger man who had been invited to live in his home. This was no week-end visit. We had nowhere else to go.

We all tried very hard to live happily together. Steve and I even adopted a small black and white mongrel from a local Pet Rescue Centre in an attempt to 'settle down'. We tried to care for my father, whilst seeing to it that he kept his privacy and freedom. But as the two men began to be real with each other, inevitable differences arose, sometimes centering on me, and neither could really understand the position, or role, of the other. My father, well into his seventies, still could not fathom Steve's sudden, insecure, violent outbursts, and Steve became convinced that he did not like him at all, nor want him in his home in the first place. Our bid for 'normal' life effectively ended after I had to return the dog to the Rescue Centre as Steve had become too ill and distracted to help train or care for it. Now he was coping with a resurgence of pain from his stomach ulcer, but he aggravated it by drinking spirits whenever he could. He began to spend days in our largish bedroom, only emerging in the evenings. Again our life began to exist mainly in one room, albeit large and in the middle of a pleasant flat. Again, there was the small TV and video recorder in the corner, Steve's world re-created.

Soon after we'd arrived at our new base, Steve had gone to the nearest Doctor's Surgery and declared himself a registered drug addict.

"I know, Piggie, that I have to come off drugs. I don't really want to die...I have to come off, for myself...and for you."

So it was that God's provision for us now was an alert young doctor with a compassionate heart and an iron discipline. Dr. Fisher won Steve's respect by his complete lack of fear, and constant supportive attitude towards us both. This doctor did not suffer fools or addicts gladly, but was completely uncompromising in his own stand of non-judgmental mercy. He drew up a plan of drug withdrawal for Steve on the understanding that Steve was absolutely willing to abide by that plan. There was to be no change of plan, no illegal methadone prescriptions, no bending of his will to Steve's by threat or intimidation, whatever the circumstances. He examined Steve thoroughly and left him in no doubt that if he didn't go forward with this course of action he would either die very soon, or I would leave him.

"Jenny wouldn't leave me," Steve said instantly; "she's a Christian."

I watched Dr. Fisher lean over his desk, seriously.

"Steve, I've seen all this before. I've seen people, even in relationships like this, lying in the gutter." Steve blinked. I was astonished; but I realized he was trying to strengthen the only lever he had: our relationship, to put pressure on Steve. There was no room or time for complacency. He must stick to the withdrawal programme. Steve was prescribed a certain number of methadone tablets a week, and no more. It was entirely his choice when he took them, but he was committed to reporting back to Dr. Fisher at the end of each week. At first the tablets disappeared in the next few days after the prescription, along with a bottle of Bacardi rum, but gradually, as Steve came to trust this doctor, he took the right amount of tablets each day. He even allowed me to take charge of the remainder, which I often hid. Dr. Fisher also prescribed some calming tablets for Steve's stomach problem, and began to look into the possibility of the right anti-depressant drug for him. This was more than anyone had been prepared to do for us before, and Steve's respect for Dr. Fisher resulted in his making a great effort to keep to the programme they had both agreed upon. He gave us both hope.

As one form of chemical dependency was cut down, Steve inevitably began to rely more heavily on the other, alcohol. He was bored, lonely, and he felt rejected by my father, and sometimes by me. Now I had to divide my time between caring for him and for my elderly father, who was rapidly becoming more confused and disorientated. Steve spent many hours alone in our bedroom with only music tapes or the TV for company. His body grew weaker as he lay in bed; he often lost the will to get up in the evening at all and be sociable. My father knew he was ill, but he never really comprehended why. He was puzzled and muddled by age; he could not understand the wild moods, and he grew to be relieved that his son-in-law spent so much time away from him. Steve sensed this, and his loneliness increased. He would begin drinking a bottle of Bacardi at mid-day (a time he set), and continue drinking for the rest of the day, as he watched TV or listened to his beloved music. He would be drunk by ten o'clock at night, often demanding that I go and buy him another half bottle. The times I did, I managed to drink a good half of it myself, so there was only the remaining quarter before he slumped into unconsciousness. I looked upon this as 'mercy drinking'. The times he didn't sleep, he would pad into the dark, silent lounge, and drink the whiskey in the sideboard. Terror was again at my elbow. But God had not left us at all. In fact, far from it. When he was sober, Steve would say to me, with a note of desperation in his voice,

"I wish He'd leave me alone…"

"What do you mean?" I asked.

"God won't go away…He won't go away…" He went on slowly to tell me of an image, which had come into his head, of Jesus standing between him and Satan.

"What did Jesus look like?" I asked greedily. He paused, puzzled, trying to find the words.

"I…I don't know. He had His back to me. But He had very broad shoulders."

*"For I know that my Redeemer lives…I shall see God…Whom I
shall see on my side…."*
(Job 19 v25,27)

*"No revolution will come in time to alter this man's life…except,
the one surprise of being loved."*
(Sydney Carter)

Chapter 21

As my husband and my father circled each other, like lonely planets, I struggled in the centre of aloneness, striving to bring order to our days. I gained an illusion of control by timing the events of the day, and creating my own private timetable. The basics of this were the meals to be prepared for the two men, and the shopping trips to buy food for the meals. Prayer played quite a large part in my timetable, 'arrow' prayers, agonized demands, faithless prayer, and the steady sort that illuminated the knowledge that God knew all about my situation and remained with me in it.

I would shop in my usual speedy frenzy of anxiety, racing against time, for I could never be sure that Steve wouldn't get out of bed and embark upon some altered mind adventure around the flat. My father was old, a little fearful, and at risk. Dr. Fisher had inspired Steve's will in the drug withdrawal programme, and Steve was doing his best, but both men were well aware of the dangers and temptations open to an addict. For example,

London was a mere twenty miles away by train, and nearer home there were pubs that would produce all the illegal drugs a well-practised Steve could get. He might have found the energy to try either option. He resisted the temptation.

Coupled with these, my father had his own medication sitting by his bed, deadly (with alcohol), tranquilizing tablets. I had experienced the results of this combination in Steve many times. I took to concealing these, too. Yet, ironically, it was I who appropriated some of these for Steve the mornings he was so distressed with withdrawal symptoms and despair, because although not touching him much physically, they calmed him psychologically. My attempt at giving peace was short lived. Coupled with a bottle of Bacardi rum the tablets were soon producing bizarre effects. Drunk by nightfall, Steve completely flattened a metal waste bin, absolutely convinced it was a monster coming to attack me. At other times loving caresses for me turned into dangerous commando-style strangleholds. These had been taught him by his real father many years ago, in an attempt to confirm in his son's mind that his dad did belong to SAS.

The terror I experienced has no name, nor my gratitude to God that He saved me from each assault. The darkness increased when the videos that Steve and I watched, to allay boredom and pain, were either murder stories or horror films. Each day video shops were now vying with each other for the most sensational films. Censorship seemed to be buckling.

Often danger was most acute late at night, and my reaction to it was sheer fury. I didn't know at the time that anger is the best survival mechanism that exists. Steve would sense my rage through his alcohol and chemical haze, and not understand. He became more determined, alienated and furious himself. Our rows were short and dark, the morning bringing forgetfulness for him, and exhaustion for me. He had managed to clip his intake of methadone tablets to a few a week. Sometimes he could make it to the surgery to collect his next prescription, sometimes I went for him. We often went together. It was difficult watching him sitting in the waiting room, hardly able to sit still, often sweating profusely, aware of the eyes of other patients glancing at him awkwardly. I would sit determinedly beside him, silently daring comment. Eventually, Dr. Fisher gave us permission to wait in a quiet corridor near his room, which ended the humiliation and discomfort. He would listen intently to Steve, but never pull any punches about the difficulty of the thing they were attempting to do, the pain of withdrawal for an addict (and family), or any of the psychological problems that might result. Steve felt he had a friend. He decided to give Dr. Fisher his cherished gold pen as a gift. At last I felt I had an ally who often leant very heavily on my support to control and inspire his patient. Sometimes the burden felt crushing.

Yet Dr. Fisher kept a close expert eye on my condition, too, a fact I did not fully realize at the time. I was tired. I appreciated his kindness. No other doctor had ever accepted and supported us both; it was a risk. (No-one had combined support with my anti depressant tablets before.) Under Dr. Fisher's influence Steve spent some days in a local hospital being assessed for depression and the condition of his stomach problem. He emerged with anti-depressant tablets that proved helpful to him, and medication to calm his stomach. Previously, Steve had lost count of the number of psychiatrists he'd seen, or the number of Drug Dependency Units he'd tried. Now, because someone obviously cared, he submitted himself again to the medical system that disliked him, in order to achieve a goal he had set himself. I knew God was at work again in our lives. These were the truths that upheld me as the violent behaviour ebbed and flowed. Steve struggled to survive as a person, to retain shreds of dignity and normality. As the methadone tablets decreased, so his pain increased. One night, in an effort to prolong the short time of pleasure he was having, he went into the lounge and opened my father's last whiskey bottle. My father had long since retired for the night. It was the only bottle in the sideboard as I'd removed the others weeks ago. All my fear and fury combined in a single dash to prevent him drinking the whiskey, as it was the one drink that provoked real evil. I was too late. After a bottle and a half of Bacardi rum, slugs of whiskey completed the work of the enemy. As I desperately tried to retrieve the bottle, I found myself hurled across the room, and the next minute Steve's hands were around my throat. There was only one thing left to say, and I had seconds to say it.

"In the Name of Jesus…..leave me alone!" A dazed, confused look came over his face. His hands dropped straight away. At that moment I heard my father asking uncertainly from the door,

"Are you all right?"

"No!…I'm NOT," I gasped uncharacteristically.

"That's it," Steve decided the next day, "I might have killed you, Piggie. No more whiskey." He was mortified, and not a little frightened, and was as good as his word. He re-set his plan, and decided on a very slow bottle of Bacardi every other day. He knew how to make a bottle last. I would wake on the alcohol-free days with a terrified heart, often sweating with fear as I dressed. I dreaded hearing the quiet, plaintive plea from the bed, which had the power to make me go physically hot and cold.

"I can't make it today, Piggie. Could you bring me a bottle back from the shops, please?"

Yet more often than not Steve was able to keep to the plan he had made, which was a victory in itself. There were good days when we laughed together, ate well, slept, and watched quality films on our small TV when my father was resting. We drew strength from these times, Sam sitting solemnly between us on the bed. He had been joined now by a small bright green toy dragon we called Dino. Dino was a complete tearaway. If anything went wrong it was always Dino's fault. He was very disobedient. He would steal sweets, swear, fight, and hide our most precious possessions in the bed. He made Steve smile a lot, but drove Sam to despair. He often ended up protesting loudly beneath one large furry paw. Like Arnie (who had stayed in Brighton guarding the fridge), Dino never got any dinner at all.

There were bad days, when Steve's fear and despair would soar, my pain interlinked. Once I caught him inhaling lighter fuel, and once broken ribs were the result of my expressing my anger when his fury erupted from a drunken rage. Somehow our struggle was contained without my father realizing the extent of the battle going on under his nose. A minor miracle. The faithful love of God held us all tightly. It was larger than our rows, our self will, our pain and anger. The enemy was muzzled.

"I built my house by the sea.
Not on the sands, mind you,
Not on the shifting sand.
And I built it of rock.
A strong house by a strong sea."
(Carol Bailock, Chile `75)

Chapter 22

In the very centre of the pressure of anxiety each day, God was far from silent. Quietly He would place strengthening pictures of encouragement in my mind. I saw myself as a small donkey with heavy pannier loads, yet a tall man (Jesus) had a firm hold on the donkey's bridle, and was leading it carefully along the road. Another image was of the previously wild, bucking horse I'd recognized as Steve. Now he was a controlled silent horse standing still submissively, trusting, as his Master caressed his head and spoke in his ears. There was no rope, and this horse had a saddle and a bridle. Yet, the days were long. I was often tired and irritable after caring for my father. A miserable Steve was easy prey for my snappy remarks. I remember one particular row centred on the amount of time I spent with my father. I simply yelled at Steve in frustration and weariness,

"I LIVE for you!" He regarded me thoughtfully for a moment, as if weighing that, and then responded slowly.

"I know you're telling the truth Piggie, you're crying." He sounded so sad, I wept afresh. He put his arms round me, after I had put my exhaustion with the whole situation into words that stumbled.

"These things," he said softly, "take time…"

Shortly after this, Steve suddenly announced he was going to help me with the shopping. He slept for hours after we returned from that first shopping trip, but I felt as if the sun was streaming through grey clouds. Then, when he was able, he began to work on his weakened muscles and walk for longer distances, sometimes in grim silence, sometimes with flashes of his old ridiculous humour. Dr. Fisher continued to encourage and support, affirming each positive step, and Steve's progress delighted me. And then one day, there were no more methadone tablets. Victory was very sweet indeed. Now, it was Kaolin and Morphine that calmed Steve's stomach and helped him psychologically to maintain stability, under the watchful eye of Dr. Fisher. One night, after Steve had drunk his usual bottle of Bacardi very slowly throughout the day, he suffered a complete blackout. It was then that he decided he would not drink spirits any more; and he never did. To me, this was a miracle. I felt the most incredible pride and exultation as Steve would now wheel a shopping trolley round our local supermarket, straight past every bottle shelf in the off licence section. All we bought were the few cans of brown ale Dr. Fisher permitted. We'd choose an appropriate meal for the evening, which Steve would often cook himself. A new rapport began to build between him and my father, who also loved his food. Some closeness was re-established. Steve would sit quietly with his Brown Ale listening to my father talk, smiling gently at me, and giving me an occasional wink.

There was quite a cost for this new, subdued lifestyle. Alcohol and drug withdrawal can only be fully understood by those who attempt it. Often Steve was unable to sleep at night, or he'd wake shivering and sweating, his whole being rebelling from years of abuse. His stomach ulcer protested when he ate the wrong things, the sickness continued. Now he would bring up bile...and blood. He would often have violent toothache too, yet he refused to go to a Dentist. He'd been diagnosed at last as suffering from a depressive illness, and the right anti-depressants battled to lift his moods. Some days he would sleep, others he'd be unable to sit or lie still at all, because of restless twitching muscles all over his body. Dr. Fisher continued to see us weekly. Now he began encouraging us to enjoy our free time together, away from the flat. I felt the two men were sharing some sort of understanding I didn't enter. Steve would leave these sessions thoughtful, and hold my hand all the way home from the Surgery. Once Dr. Fisher was quite open about the situation he thought we were in.

"I don't know how much time there is," he said candidly, "make the most of the time you have." Frozen with horror, I chose to forget this remark, breathless with the unthinkable. God had promised healing. I banished the words to the lowest recesses of my being, and piled hope on top of them, like rocks.

Watching a strangely good science fiction film one night, with Sam and Dino, one particular scene transfixed us. The hero, from another planet, was outraged when a deer was hunted, shot, and tied to the front of the hunters` jeep in mid America. The hero immediately placed his hands on the lifeless animal, and as power rushed through him, the still body suddenly began to jerk and twitch. The man pulled the ropes away, lifted the deer free, and threw the kicking animal gently towards the forest. It was all done in a single victorious movement. The deer bounded away. My hand met Steve's on the video control at exactly the same moment. We didn't say a word, but watched that particular scene over and over again. Something neither of us could explain was catching our hearts.

In our brief travels to the shops and back, we'd met the Minister of the local Free Church. He had somehow managed to communicate care to a silent, surly Steve, and he overcame that distrust of strangers who visited the flat. Tom was invited to come and share Communion with us one day during my father's rest time.

At first I sat rigid and tense as Steve and Tom talked, half expecting Steve to explode from self-consciousness and fear. But Tom fielded the irritability with quiet courtesy and great humility. Soon we were praying together and sharing bread and wine. I felt God's Holy Spirit come gently, but with power. I was filled with joy and felt a strong peace inside me. There was a silence. I glanced at Steve. He seemed to be struggling for words, our visitor all but forgotten. Eventually he lapsed into the language of a culture he knew best.

"Man, that was incredible…"

"What was, Steve?" I asked. He looked dazed, almost incoherent.

"Well…I've never felt like that before. Man…I don't suppose you'd understand. You've never had a hit before. But THAT…just then I felt as if I was having…well, the feeling all over my body...It was incredible. It was better than a hit." Jesus was drawing him closer.

"Let not your heart be troubled…trust in God , trust also in Me. For in my Father's house are many mansions. If it were not so I would have told you. I am going there to prepare a place for you."
(John 14 v 1-3 RSV)

"Teach my boy that at the side of the everlasting 'why?' is a YES!...YES!...YES!" – (Mr Emerson – 'Room with a view')

Chapter 23

For a year Steve neither drank spirits nor took illegal drugs. It was a victory not unmixed with sadness; somehow life felt unfulfilled for both of us, as we tried to care for my father, and for each other. Although Steve moved freely through a day now, accomplishing tasks and achieving a form of normality, he was quieter and more subdued than I'd ever known him. He still had very low moods. He'd lost weight and I teased him about his stylish new haircut, yet his sadness disturbed me. I felt a strangeness I couldn't identify as I watched this calm, good-looking man walking obediently to the Surgery each week to report to Dr. Fisher. He was almost disturbingly normal. The old humour only appearing now and again after a few brown ales. I saw an enveloping inexpressible sadness that I could not touch, or explain.

It was now that my own ability to cope seemed to be getting worse. My father's confusion was increasing with age, and I was frequently filled with great panic. Prayer certainly didn't stop my feelings or allay them. I was constantly tired and angry. At least once a month I would rage at whoever would listen to me that I 'needed some help'. The problem was, I had no idea what sort of help I meant, or who was best qualified to give it. Tablets failed to make an impression upon me. I remember shopping one day with Steve and waiting as he selected a pair of jeans he needed. I wanted to tear up every pair on the rack, and stand and scream. My body felt as if it was falling apart, yet I felt disconnected with all around. I hung on with a great effort. Once home, I lay down on the bed knowing with great clarity that I could not continue to function in the same way much longer without collapse.

Steve was patient and grumpy with me by turns. He would cook me my most favourite meal in the world when I was particularly weepy. This was a northern dish his grandmother had perfected. It was intricate to prepare, involving pineapple chunks, mince, baked beans, and onions, an odd mixture, but which tasted the nearest thing to manna to me. I loved him for doing this because he would often now be exhausted with the effort, and completely unable to eat any of it himself because it was so rich.

Christmas approached again, and my fear heightened. In the past this had meant a huge stockpiling of bottles, and the prospect of days of alcoholic lunacy. I was wondering if the new life style would hold firm. Soon I was swept into Christmas preparations which incorporated those of my father, and my anxieties were buried under a mound of food shopping, card writing and decorations. I did, however, notice gratefully that it was only cans of brown ale that Steve stored away for the festivities. He also bought the ingredients for my own favourite non-alcoholic drinks, and a liqueur we both enjoyed. He took care with these things, and soon began teasing me mysteriously about my Christmas present. I'd not seen this depth of thoughtfulness in the preparation for previous Christmas times. We both began to relax more and enjoy the pre-Christmas films on the TV. And when I was still enough, I would feel God's pleasure and encouragement in the change in our lives. His concern was, as ever, for our good. I would be calmed and strengthened by an awareness of His presence.

One night, after my father had gone to bed, we wrapped our presents and put the finishing touches to the Christmas tree. As it grew late, I suggested that we go to bed. I was a little concerned about the amount of brown ale Steve had drunk. I always felt easier when he was lying down having taken his evening tablets. He'd enjoyed our time and his drink, and was unusually expressive as we prepared for bed.

"Piggie, no one knows how much I love you. I love you more than I've ever loved anyone in my life..." I glance up a bit tiredly at the unsteady figure, used to drink speaking.

"Thank you...I love you too..." It was almost an effort to say it. Efficiently as ever, I took the required tablets out of their different bottles as he climbed into bed. Anti-depressants, sleeping tablets and tablets to neutralize stomach acid. It was a familiar routine. I handed him a glass of water.

"Get these down you! There's only five..."

"I wish there were fifty," he muttered suddenly, with a great longing sadness. I ignored the stab of pain, undressed and jumped into bed, praying he would soon be asleep.

Twenty minutes later he began to whimper, then that changed into great moans. I froze, from years of knowing this to be the best policy, and listened carefully. He sounded just like a child confronted with its greatest fear, and helpless to escape. The sound was full of deep dread and pain, a regret that was almost despair. After a while there was silence, and I slipped gratefully into a dreamless sleep.

I woke suddenly at midnight, as if shaken. I was awake instantly. The room felt strange. I couldn't think for a moment what was wrong, and then I realized it was the silence. There was no sound of Steve breathing. I listened concentrating, but I could hear none. Taking a deep breath I kicked him hard on the shin. There was no responding roar of fury. I leapt round to his side of the bed. There was no answer to my calls. Quickly, I switched on the bedside light. He was lying relaxed in his favourite position, apparently asleep, his head resting comfortably on his arm. He looked very peaceful, but he didn't respond at all when I shook him, or when I tried to heave him into a sitting position. As I attempted this with terrified strength, his jaw dropped. Then I knew something was very wrong. I fled into the lounge and phoned for an ambulance. When they arrived a short while later, the paramedics listened to my account of events, and soon began working on Steve on the bedroom floor. Oddly, I remember thinking how handsome he looked, and how glad I was that he was partially clothed. I watched fearful, immobilized as they eventually carried him to the ambulance. It was then that a second ambulance arrived, and I had my transport to the hospital. A quarter of an hour later, after a noisy dash through the darkness, I caught a glimpse of Steve on a trolley being rushed into the casualty department. People were running alongside, and there was a red blanket pulled up over his face. I could see only a mop of dark hair. Jumping from my ambulance, I reasoned that he must be cold, so they had covered him up. The nice nurse in the small side room gave me a cup of tea. I registered that this must be serious; tea wasn't usual on our hospital visits. She was very gentle. She asked how long we'd been married, and suddenly it was difficult for me to answer because nothing seemed to be making any sense at all. Soon, a ward sister appeared, followed by an Indian doctor.

"Is he all right?" I heard myself ask. She paused.

"I'm afraid we have some bad news for you. Your husband died. He died in the ambulance. We tried to bring him back, but we couldn't."

Suddenly, she seemed to be at the wrong end of a telescope.

"I am sorry." Everything went into slow motion. I couldn't understand why she kept staring at me. The nice nurse was even more gentle.

"Can we phone anyone for you?" No, they couldn't do that. They called a taxi because I seemed to be in a strange trance-like state, barely in contact with reality.

"Do you have a faith?" the concerned nurse asked suddenly.

"Yes...yes, I do...," I said with great force.

"That's good," she said, "because you're going to need it."

KIDSTUFF

"When I was a child
I could never see the point of the heroine
She was always feeble
She screamed a lot
She got captured
And was taken to a very high tower
Someone always came in the end.

When I was a child
Someone made me see the point of the heroine
I was always feeble
I screamed a lot
I got captured
I'm in a high tower
Someone may come in the end."
(Stewart Henderson/'Assembled in Britain')
`86

Chapter 24

The best defence mechanism against grief is supposed to be denial. It was very hard to feel anything except trance-like shock in those first few hours, even days, after Steve died. I remember sitting on his side of the bed back home and weeping more from shock than anything else. In my head I could hear him saying, 'Don't cry, Piglet'. But there was nothing else left to do.

In this bewildered state I continued to care for my father, the caring minister, Dave, making frequent visits. There was much to organize before the funeral, which seemed to keep my grief in check. There was to be a post mortem because no-one knew exactly why Steve had died so suddenly. However, God knew. A few nights later, I was praying desperately. I was asking the inevitable question…'why?'I sensed that I was to turn to John 14:1-2. As I read the words I saw clearly another word on the page, above the printed ones. The printed words read 'trust in God, and trust in Me…' the one above them, was, 'RESCUE'. It was my answer. I felt instant relief. Steve's death was a rescue. Years later I was to realize how much of a rescue it was for me too, but I did not see that then.

Dr. Fisher was distraught.

"What happened? What happened?...." I could hear the shock in his voice on the telephone. I struggled to outline what had happened.

"Look, come and see me. Don't wait in the waiting room. Just tell them, and come in."

He was literally pacing the floor of his room when I walked in, his face troubled. I appreciated him all over again.

"Jenny, I'm so sorry. We were doing so well...What did happen?" He listened as carefully as ever as I tried to tell him.

"How many cans of beer do you think Steve drank?"

"Eleven." I replied promptly. He rolled his eyes heavenwards.

"He thought his body had the same tolerance, you see. He didn't realize it didn't any more..." He sat down suddenly at his desk opposite me, and was still. "Steve had some very good points....Our job has been to support him and help him survive on less harmful drugs. We've failed. He had so much. He had you. But it wasn't enough. He couldn't quite make it." He still looked upset. I told him how much Steve had appreciated him, and gave him the gold pen. He accepted it quietly.

"He had many admirable qualities..." He placed the pen down, and looked at me in his usual way that mixed compassion with business. "Now...how are you doing...?"

I was coping. I was living mindlessly. I was simply occupying myself with tasks. I did everything I had to do, connected with the funeral, completely automatically. Caring for my bewildered father was a tiring, mixed blessing. I had no energy to feel or do anything more.

I remembered the words of scripture that had seemed right to put on our wedding invitations those years ago.

"Many waters cannot quench love, neither can floods drown it...for love is as strong as death." (Song of Songs 8:6, 7) It was these that I had inscribed on Steve's headstone months later. I believed love had been the overcomer in our life together, and remained that. I loved Steve no less now that he was dead, and I felt his love for me was the same. It was this inescapable fact that shone for me in the darkest moments of grief: I did not have to stop loving him. I was angry; I was furious with him for dying; I was angry to be alone, but I felt strangely assured that he was 'safe'...as Jesus promises (John 17:12).

Psalm 12 :5 speaks of this safety too:

"I will now arise, says the Lord, and place him in the safety for which he longs."It was clear to me that Steve was completely free, now, to love, and to know the Saviour who had called and drawn him to Himself. The stallion was ready, and had been ridden away. God had not only heard my prayers that He draw Steve closer to Him; He had answered them. But he had done it in a way I couldn't possibly have imagined, or expected, or even wanted. He had kept His promise, and healed my husband. A total healing.

It was later the pain came. The unuttered scream that I'd managed to contain at Steve's funeral erupted in nights of tears. I loved him so much – and he was gone. I knew where he was, but that didn't stop the pain I felt. I shouted at my father. I yelled at God. As shock and numbness wore off, I seemed to be in a land full of physical heaviness, emptiness, and abandonment. I had no map for this land. I had not been here before. Even now the memories of this land seem too painful to examine, and the details are blurred and buried in time. Yet the God who heals gently confronts me afresh, and I weep to be healed. The shining strength is the truth that Steve is completely healed, at long last.

As in the picture I'd seen years previously, the joyful Dalmatian was now capering along at the heels of his Master. God had answered Steve's heart cry, 'Why can't I feel like this all the time?' He had replaced agony with ecstasy, and rescued us both. Through my tears, I knew the nurse had been right. I did need my faith. But I could take heart; Jesus had overcome my suffering, and would reveal His glory in and through it all.

The official cause of death was stated as 'Mixed drug poisoning'. Dr. Fisher had been right; Steve's body had simply given up. I was deeply thankful the verdict was not a suicide one, as I would have found that intolerable. No-one had known Steve would die then, least of all himself. As the days moved on, I would sleep at nights holding Sam close. His head became quite worn with pressure and tears. My moods swung wildly from inexpressible anger to robotic numbness. I washed down the walls of our bedroom and cursed Steve quite roundly as all the brown nicotine slid onto the cloth, leaving white wall beneath. I would often think I would hear his voice, and I'd wait stupidly for him to appear when anyone came to the door of the flat, with a mixture of dread and anticipation. There were days when I felt physically ill and dead within, and my only prayer to God was `Help me`…Very soon I became depressed and staggered through everyday routine aided by tablets from a supportive Dr. Fisher.

Then very, very, slowly a slender scaffolding of hope began to grow within my innermost being. Beauty still existed. I was free. The world was still there. I no longer felt my insides were a crumbling aching mess every day. Then came points in my days when I didn't want to scream at people, or weep.All I could do was live one day at a time, held in the familiar routine of caring for my father. I would be grateful to God for getting through each day. I inched along a switchback of emotions, the predominant one an awareness of my aloneness. I knew that God was with me in my bereavement, and much peace came from simply sitting quietly on my own with Him. Once, I had the oddest feeling that the whole time with Steve had been observed indeed by many, many people ('a cloud of witnesses'... Heb.12:1). I didn't know them, but they now stood cheering and offering me encouragement. I could not make head or tail of this, and wondered at the time about my sanity, but this picture is perfectly in line with Scripture. Gradually each day began to become precious, not least because I had lived through it, and the caring support of a local Christian Fellowship enfolded me with love and hope for the future.

"The first step in treatment for trauma is to fine a place of safety." (James Thompson/Trauma Specialist)

Fifteen years later, I have been brought gradually face to face again with all the pain of the past by a loving, healing God, who continues to work in my life by His unchanging Spirit. Now I can see that my role, not Steve's, was that of the stronger tree in the prophetic picture given before our wedding. We did indeed grow side by side, roots pushing deeper into the soil as we learned about growing, and the utter dependability of that soil. We had been shaken by storms but had not fallen. We had both experienced love and belonging in a way that would have been impossible if we had not met. Perhaps that was God's plan. A selfish, opinionated, middle-class woman had her religion extracted, and replaced with reality, part of which was learning to respond to the real needs of another...not what she imagined they were. A desperate, alienated Northerner learnt that his toughness was no shield for his longing to be loved and valued for whom he really was; and he was forced into change because of a supernatural love that would not give up.

Months after the funeral I put the statue of a small puppy on Steve's grave; he'd always wanted a dog. I often smile to myself as I imagine his response.

"Bloody soppy woman..." But God made and chose me, as He did Steve, for who we were when we were together, and I believe He gave us both the strength and protection for that time. And all those days will continue to affect and mould my life in one way or another. I choose to hope it is for good, for continued change and growth in me, and perhaps in others. All there is left to do is echo Steve's heart in the words of Job, and experience their truth:

"Oh that my words were written!

Oh that they were inscribed in a book.

Oh, that with an iron pen and lead they were graven in the rock forever!

For I know that my Redeemer lives....

I shall see God."

(Job 19 v 23-27 RSV)

An old Indian Prayer:
"When I am dead
Cry for me a little.
Think of me sometimes
But not too much.
Think of me now and again
As I was in life.
At some moments it's pleasant to recall.
But not for long.
Leave me in peace,
And I shall leave you in peace.
And while you live,
Let your thoughts be with the living."

The Strongest Tree

Part 2

"FOUR DOORS DOWN"

"Do you have a faith at all......?"
(Casualty Nurse Dec. 1990)
"Do not look to anyone else. I am your husband, lover, guide and friend"
(Word from God - Jan.1991)

Chapter 25

When travelling through a strange land it is usually wise to take a map. I had found that grief can feel exactly like a strange land, so in the uncharted roads and pathways after my husband's death I was glad of my faith. I was alone…yet not alone.

Seven years had felt like seven hundred as we had battled with his drink and drug addiction, born in childhood deprivation and nurtured in adult trauma and abuse. Others sins are much less public. Oddly, the suffering deepened our faith in remarkable ways providing the strength at last for the addictions to be relinquished. It was too late. The cost of the courage for that victory was death and a transformed life elsewhere.

Part of me died too. I felt like a wraith, abandoned in howling desert wastes. It was not that I experienced loss, rage and guilt: I was loss, consumed by grief and scattered like ashes.

Then my immediate identity became again that of a carer, for my father was now in his eighties and in need of my support. It was this practical framework of routine that began to give my own recovery shape.

I inched forward through those hideous days and months trying not to think too deeply, and at the same time stricken by periods of forgetfulness. I often sat alone in silence, sometimes for long stretches of time. I listened and listened.

I could almost feel my shattered being knitting together in the peace.

Gradually I became able to drag myself free from the quicksand of bereavement. Healing does take its own time, and I needed the gifts of patience and trust to know that there is life after death.

The grieving process was compounded by being my father's carer, for both 'cared for' and 'carer' have their unique difficulties. Both worlds are fractured and misshapen. As I wrestled with fears, resentment and rage, the kind gentleman I'd grown up with began to descend into childlike ways.

I longed to be free, and then felt crippled by guilt. I longed to be more compassionate and patient, but my own loss had left me raw and without the emotional resources I needed. It was only memories of my father, as the gentle, humorous family protector and champion of his small daughter that enabled me to cope. Yet always the same quietness, silence, listening, brought me refreshment and strength: a new direction. There was some silent communication that inspired and supported. I began to have hope.

There came the gradual appearance of landmarks in the desert, friends and safe spaces. A track appeared through the sand. When my father died some years later, I sold the flat with all its dark memories and moved into a small white bed-sit. I went to India and healing flooded my soul.

When I returned, I lived from day to day in my tiny oasis, accompanied, as ever, by the quietness. As I had no idea what shape or form a new life-would take, the trick was in surviving the past and existing each day.

I cried into the quietness about being alone, yet I wanted to be obedient. I knew God was my salvation. From the centre of peace came an answer.

"I will satisfy the desires of your heart. Do not despair. I do not work in the ways man works. I will meet every need you have, including this one. I have begun. Do not be afraid. I am not confined by your mind. I work my will on the stars and planets. I am able. Peace"

Chapter 26

Aloneness gradually became more of an ally than an enemy. I continued to live from one blank day to the next in my small white bed sit for over a year.

"Why don't you tell God what you'd like, what you desire?" suggested Jessica, my Brighton friend. The idea appealed to me so I sat on a rug on the floor and asked the Almighty for a husband, a dog, and a cottage with an open fire. I felt sure He would sift the gold from the dross, yet time passed without any clear direction of where I was to make my home.

The answer appeared quite unexpectedly, as these things often do. A young couple, who attended my Church, gave me the key to a flat they had just viewed in their own house hunting.

"We felt this was more for you than it was for us."

They were right. Whilst not a cottage, the place was a spacious maisonette near a park. So I left my tiny sanctuary and moved into the maisonette. It was beautiful.

For some reason the previous owners had completely redecorated and refurbished the place before moving out and for months I'd tip toe around quite overcome. There was a gleaming bathroom, large lounge with an open fire place, two bedrooms, and huge picture windows overlooking a pretty communal garden. Light poured into the place, and it seemed to pour into me too. I kept thinking irrationally that the owner would appear and demand the flat back. I was half afraid it would disappear. Now, after years of ugly bed sit furniture arranged by someone else, or even familiar family furniture, waxed with dark memories, I was free to choose my own environment. I felt this a big responsibility. I couldn't afford to furnish the flat with the exquisite taste that my father had demonstrated in our family flat, but I did have his appreciation of beauty and design.

One day as I rode through Watford on the top deck of a bus I spotted a stately pine dresser in a shop window. When I went to buy it I discovered there were matching table and chairs on special offer! The sense of joy and freedom was exhilarating, and when they were delivered, and in place, I sat down and wept. Empowered, I put some blue willow pattern plates on the dresser, and ordered some dark blue velvet floor length curtains for the picture windows. Then my nerve disappeared in a flurry of doubt. I phoned a friend.

"I'm not sure if this looks all right?"

"Of course it's all right. It sounds lovely."

"But you haven't seen it..."

"I don't have to, Jenny. You've got very good taste."

I felt astonished. Then I began to realize that part of my identity had been submerged by years of pain and abuse. Restoration had come.

I'd sit curled up in a big armchair for hours, letting time drift, just watching the bright blue window full of sky and changing clouds. It was a blue green velvet armchair, a gift that toned with the curtains. I'd look at waving cherry tree branches, birds, the attractive garden, and revel in freedom and peace. For to me, what had felt like hundreds of years of despair and blackness had melted into joy. I had not brought that about myself at all. I had nothing to do with it. I'd only trusted sometimes that all was for a purpose, but then I'd been given that capacity too. A new day had dawned. I was at liberty!

There was, inevitably, a residue of the suffering still alive within me. I experienced flashbacks, nightmares, and anxiety attacks, but slowly, bodily and mental pain became more manageable. I knew the storms would pass. Thus with a degree of control back in my life, and a safe place to live, the healing could continue.

The days began as ever, sitting quietly, listening. I'd pray and then move out from experienced love to be creative and try to live more fully. My spacious place, within and without was bringing life.

"I think your home is your castle," sniffed one indignant acquaintance who failed to gain admittance to my fortress. It was indeed. The drawbridge was forever going to remain up and closed, or at the very least, completely under my control! There was no way I wanted to admit anyone to my deepest self ever again. Days passed. I became a new creation that the old would not have recognized at all.

Chapter 27

I had begun to notice that people came to me and talked (I mean beyond the call of courtesy!).I realized I must have inherited my parents listening skills and decided I would train to become a counsellor. So I found myself a Course, a Therapist, quite a bit of courage and began. As I trained, a new world rolled open before me, and I began to co operate fully with my own growth as a person. I discovered power and dignity, totally new feelings for a trauma victim. Now no longer helpless I could return often to my past frightening experiences from a position of safety and understanding. Through thought, prayer, and expert therapy, I learnt I could often rework my pain into facilitating healing for others. I liked God's plan. It meant, of course that my suffering had not been meaningless at all. I found this empowering in itself, for through grace I had become a catalyst for recovery.

After I qualified in my chosen field, I joined a local group of counsellors to deepen and extend my learning.

One afternoon, during a break in our monthly meeting, I noticed an open magazine on a nearby chair. The face of a well known Christian author and speaker smiled up at me. It is extraordinary how such chances can hinge change. I picked up the magazine and read the article. The author had undertaken the specialized pastoral care in which I was interested. A spark of recognition flared in me as I read. I wrote to her expressing support. Some time later I was fortunate enough to meet her and become involved in the work as a counsellor on her team of helpers.

The work was demanding, but very rewarding. From time to time the team would meet together socially for an exchange of news and views, support and encouragement. I was sipping a fruit juice and munching crisps at one such gathering, when a snippet of conversation detached itself from the general buzz of conversation and fell on my ears with the force akin to a grenade. Someone spoke the name of the small sea side town where they lived. I literally jumped. It was exactly the same place where I'd spent many holidays with my parents over thirty years ago. The memories were so special that I had even returned there once for a holiday on my own. Almost without thinking I found myself standing opposite the lady who had just spoken. I did not know her well.

"I heard where you live…" I began rather breathlessly.

"Why don't you come and stay with me sometime?" she said with a lovely smile, "You'd be most welcome".

Sea-side sights and sounds sang to me as I strolled down the main street of the town. Bittersweet memories gusted from the sea. The Greensward seemed smaller. The cosy cafe where we'd feasted on fish and chips as a family had changed ownership. Even the quaint repertory theatre, our summer evening delight, had new management and over thirty years had re-fashioned my life too. I almost expected to see my parents stepping over the springy grass above the beach from. In my mind's eye I saw my father again, exulting in each stride, relishing the clean air after his work in London. Now I could see the beach huts standing in a stiff row, like soldiers along the shoreline. There was my mother, brown as a berry, leaning out of our hut, chatting happily to the folk next door. Her fashionable bathing costume exhibited a pair of beautifully shaped legs. What a shame neither ever became the remotest bit wet! Somewhere there, notebook in hand, lounged a rather bored teenager, irritated that the wind was ruffling her carefully arranged dark hair.

Suddenly my exquisite sadness broke into a wave of joy. This was the last place we had been truly content as a family; it would always be a very special place indeed.

I had accepted Carol's invitation to stay with her, and as we talked I found myself sharing memories and ideas. I remember her thoughtful look.

"Jenny, you're thinking of returning here. If God put those desires in your heart in the first place, why do you think He doesn't want to meet them?"

She was wondering why living in the town was only my dream. Why couldn't it come true? I gasped in amazement. I had the odd sensation of a door opening....
somewhere.

Later, I walked again along the sea front.

"Do you want me to come here?" I asked God. Past the steep wooden steps to the water. Past the beach huts. I listened. And then I listened,...and listened. Then to my astonishment huge tears began to well up behind my sunglasses and slide down my cheeks. The glasses slithered onto the bridge of my nose. Still the tears came, filling my head and heart with a great gentleness. I wasn't sad. I was certain. As I could not stop weeping I sat down on the sea wall and let the tears come. I'd read many times about the loving heart of God but never experienced it this way before. So my longing for a move was not after all 'too good to be true'. Carol had been right. I had that longing because God had put it there in the first place. He had brought me back after thirty years so that healing might continue, further rebuilding of the ancient walls that had been trampled down. I wept for the rest of the walk, not minding at all because my heart was leaping for joy.

"What on earth are you going there for, there's nothing THERE?", my next door neighbour wailed on my return. That was the whole point. I now knew the direction in which my future lay. My news continued to have a mixed reception.

"I don't even want to talk about it", exclaimed my closest friend banging a full mug of coffee down on her work surface in horror. Yet, of course, it was she who drove me backwards and forwards flat hunting. She prayed, as usual, but now for perfect timing and the right place for me to live. The week I put my home on the market a buyer appeared! Jen and I drove miles and viewed many flats. None seemed quite right.

One morning we arrived at a flat that had already been sold. The Estate Agent was red faced with embarrassment. "I am so sorry for the mix up. Um..., there does happen to be a flat for sale upstairs here. I don't know if you'd care to look at that one? It's not actually on the market yet, but..."

As soon as we turned into the enormous, airy lounge with old rose curtains, I knew I had come home. This block of flats was only yards from the sea and shops, in a long peaceful road lined with trees.

"This is the one", I declared.

"But you haven't seen round the property..."

"This is it!'

My friend and I were very excited. We anticipated our continuing friendship, now punctuated with holidays for her by the sea.

It was fortunate that I could keep the strength of my vision and joy, for when I put the wheels in motion for the buying and selling to commence, real difficulties began in earnest. The day I learnt that my offer for the flat had been accepted, the buyer for my flat pulled out. I had no option but to trust and wait, which is always far easier to contemplate spiritually than to do in reality. By a series of convoluted events which I could not grasp, and doubt that anyone else would want to, I became part of a chain of nineteen people, all of whom had to buy and sell their properties before I could contemplate my own sale and purchase.

My estate agent felt betrayed, my solicitor raged, and I felt trapped in a sinister no man's land I hadn't known existed.

For three months two sets of solicitors and estate agents waged polite but vicious war. I lived in a state of indrawn breath, sustained by prayer and strong coffee. Very occasionally a fragile lull was fractured by an informative call from an empathic neighbour.

"I've just been talking to your buyer. They say their solicitor is hopeless. Well, they don't think they'll get into your flat here in a month of Sundays... This must be so worrying for you." My insides felt like Spaghetti Junction. I telephoned solicitors, absentee landlords, surveyors and removal firms in a tortuous circle, constantly re-setting dates and times. I prayed. After all, God had made a promise. My prayer was probably without the faithfulness or conviction of that of my friend. Each day she'd contact me to offer a listening ear and some encouragement, a Scripture relevant to the moment or a funny story to lift my spirits. What was remarkable was that what she believed the exact opposite to that which everyone else believed. I hung on grimly, like a dog with a bone.

Those who live alone, as I did then, know that unshared fears and pressures can magnify, growing to menacing proportions. Vulnerability becomes like a shroud, deadening reason and common sense. Promises wither into mere words. Thus I heard again the wind of the desert howling in my ears.

"I'll be just fine staying here" I told myself one cold afternoon, trying desperately to tape draught excluder over an ill-fitting bedroom window.

"I can cope. . .I'll buy a dog..." Now faithless rebellion had begun to rise. Although I was being faithless, I was in covenant with the One who is always faithful.

I trudged on. I guess the cross must have looked pretty final. I knew I must forget the past and concentrate on each day in the positive way my faith demanded. I began to speak out to people that the exchange date for my move was set for the middle of November. The completion date was the end of the month. Then I heard that the Bank was 'pulling the plug' on the other purchaser. I stood quite still in the dark and waited. Each second felt like a year during that last day of waiting. The many hours crawled along like sick snails. Then came the all important phone call. There were ten minutes to spare to the agreed deadline. The chain of nineteen purchasers was completed.

"We only just made it in time..." crowed my solicitor.

"The whole chain has been as good as gold. It's miraculous. The flat is yours. Congratulations". She sounded surprised.

The Strongest Tree

Chapter 28

I was welcomed in style to the town. The remaining sea-side hotel boasted an unexpectedly beautiful four poster bed in which I passed my last night before the move. When I went to the estate agents the next day to collect my keys I was presented with a large bunch of flowers from the staff. It was a thoughtful gesture that meant much; we all knew that a battle had been won.

A special sea-side flat…and every foot belonged to me; every square inch! It did not take me long to unpack the huge brown removal boxes. I was soon using my new found confidence in home-making to co-ordinate colour schemes and belongings. I decided gleefully on the arrangement of each room. Over the next days I discovered a nearby second-hand furniture shop, and hunted fabrics and pictures with great joy.

I spent glorious months waking, it seemed, the moment the winter sun peeped into the bedroom. I would dress quickly and walk as fast as I could down to the sea front. Here I could gaze at the land, my promised land, spread out before me in either direction. Miles and miles edged by calm, shimmering sea. I stood enfolded by warm memories and a future life of hope. All that God's faith had dreamed had become a reality.

I would revel in the early morning quietness of the beach as the sea jumped over each breakwater. I often joined it. I would stride through the tiny wavelets looking for shells, or simply relishing my freedom. Later I walked the grassy trails overlooking the sea, the carefully manicured gardens and the paths down to the promenade. I would dream into the waves afresh and then return to my spacious flat, tired but content. I was home.

Christmas came four weeks after I arrived and I chose to remain alone. I felt continually healed by my freedom to choose after years of constraint. I relaxed in 'aloneness' and silence, somehow mysteriously rebuilt in the heart of space and rest.

It had been the Anglican church in the town that had beckoned me. I thought that I was drawn by an attractive stained glass window over the Communion Table. A sermon that the vicar preached captured exactly my own experience of life.

"Being burdened by God", he pointed out, "sometimes brings pain and sorrow. Christianity was not always sweetness and light. Mary the mother of Jesus experienced great pain. The way to belong to God was to submit to Him, body and soul, as she had, doing His will." I felt my struggles with past circumstances had been understood, almost justified. I also liked the way the preacher knelt to receive the collection bag from a small child.

Christmas morning was joyful, although I kept myself rather apart from the welcoming congregation. I politely refused offers of Christmas lunch, my peaceful refuge awaited me! The smiling vicar welcomed his new parishioner with a hug and a seasonal kiss on the cheek, even remembering my name. For some reason that was beyond me and I wept all the way back to the flat.

Over the next three years I became stronger mentally and physically. My thoughts returned to my counselling work. In a combination of prayer and grit I found a job

in the local centre for the homeless. My legs were literally weak with fear in those first days. I wondered if memories and experiences from the past would allow me to work effectively. Now I was viewing, from a safe distance, a world that had been dangerous years ago. I found I was able to contribute support in a new, informed way. I was no longer ruled by terror and pain. The pall of addiction, mental illness, and alcoholism no longer trapped or smothered me. The hope that had freed and healed now marched into other lives with an astonishing discernment and boldness.

I began to work from home and also enjoyed preaching in local Methodist churches. Old friends, my 'family', came and shared holiday days by the sea. Yet I still kept my rather uninvolved distance from others, not willing or ready to let many people into my new ordered life. Just occasionally loneliness lapped at life's edges, like the small waves beyond the Greensward, but that seemed a small price to pay for safety and power.

I felt secure, balancing work and training with interests and travel. I was well able to survive the times when all seemed too quiet, or when I saw too many families laughing together on the beach. I made one trusted Church friend laugh aloud as we enjoyed a picnic and the sea view at her beach hut.

"I love this place" I said eyeing the misty blue horizon dreamily.

"It's lovely" she agreed softly, "My husband and I were always very happy here."

"What I'd like" I continued finishing an excellent crab sandwich and accepting her offer of another, "is a dog, a beach hut and a husband". My friend laughed.

"In that order?" she asked. I grinned.

"Not necessarily."

Chapter 29

"Do you think you will get married again?"

I was at work and the question had come from a client. As it was important that I continued to hold hope for both of us, I said that I would get married. In the resulting silence I felt I had walked to the very edge of a spiritual diving board. It had been a lengthy walk to that point. Promises had been made, and although they had often grown fainter, like a mountain through the mist, they always reappeared. I was sometimes grateful for the mist, for part of me feared another relationship of deep commitment. I was in control being single; I had my own destiny in hand. Yet what a rebellious thought, for I knew Divine certainty held me, not my preferences or ideas. I was both awed and petrified.

I was at the mercy of mood swings and my own humanity.

"Where is this person, the man who is for me?" I had asked Jen angrily, one winter evening before my move.

"He'll come." She smiled with maddening calm. "Perhaps you're not ready yet."

I snorted in an unladylike way.

"Really. How do you know? I'm not sure it's possible. If you think about it, he'll have to be a psychiatrist, a social worker or a priest! No one else could cope..."

It is odd how negativity can be so compulsive.

"Well...I'm still praying". I heard the note of iron in her voice that I knew so well. "God has given me exactly what to pray".

I stopped in mid moan.

"I beg your pardon?"

It was then that this infuriating woman who had supported and encouraged me through counselling training courses, moving home, and the blackest times known to dysfunctional woman, gave a broad smile. She pulled a small red notebook from a table drawer at the end of the sofa.

I watched in amazement as she found the right page. It was obvious she'd done that many times before. She smoothed the notebook open carefully.

"I was praying for you months ago and I felt that God was giving me a list of the qualities of the man I must pray about." I thought it was time I closed my mouth at this point, so I did.

He would be..."a man of Godly authority, with leadership qualities, gentleness and humility. He's romantic and passionate, enjoying the same hobbies as you; music, art, and drama. I had the impression of a large house with a beamed frontage. The garden was not over-looked. It had mature shrubs and older trees. It seemed the house had four bedrooms, a reception room and a study". It was a rather quiet evening after that.

Life in my treasured seaside town continued in a sort of structured, fulfilled way. Sometimes, expectations would arise within me..., the hope that had fuelled the answer to my client's question about marriage. Occasionally, in my walks around the town, I would search absently for a large house with a beamed frontage. I saw no such dwelling. Rather thankfully there was no change in my life or relationships either. I became one of the founder members of a local Christian counselling group. I explained all about it to the Anglican vicar who lived four doors up the road. I was a little concerned about him as his wife had died several months previously, but I was a professional bereavement counsellor, so I knew my ground.

In 2004 Carol, the gentle lady who had welcomed me back to the town went to a Christian conference in Canada. She had long since become a friend and prayer-partner, so I awaited her return with eagerness. She arrived glowing with life and joy at a supper some friends and I gave to celebrate her return. Angels hovering about our meal table must have had their ears ringing as wonders were unfolded. Afterwards, Carol graciously prayed with each one of us as we reflected on all she had experienced of God in Canada. When she prayed with me I saw in my head, a strange tunnel at the end of which was...my own marriage. It was quite unmistakable. I was stunned into silence. I noticed Carol watching me closely.

I took a deep breath.

"I...I think I'm going to be married again "I stammered, almost unwillingly," but...I don't see how or who...

As we left that evening Carol asked me a question no one else heard.

"What about Andrew…?"

"The Vicar…? Good gracious no…" I replied hastily.

But God's Word had been released.

Chapter 30

"I wonder if I might come and have a chat with you?" The Vicar of the Parish church was very polite.

"It's a professional matter", he continued, "I wondered if I was going along the right lines recovery wise...?" I instantly clicked into full professional bereavement counsellor mode.

"Yes of course. I hope I can be of help."

A few days later I donned my super deluxe counselling persona and listened hard for nearly two hours (this wasn't, you understand, a moment to mention fees or boundaries). From my defensive position I noted that the vicar's grieving process seemed to be going as well as these things do. He was doing well. I was the one who was struggling. I worked very effectively at keeping an impartial detached edge in the proceedings, yet towards the middle of our session I was suddenly aware of an uncontrolled thumping in my chest region. It was my heart. It was curving away from me like a runaway supermarket trolley. With a great effort I became still and gentle but most straightforward in my interventions. I had often held my own feelings while counselling clients, it was a routine part of the process, but this time I needed every bit of skill I possessed. There seemed no good reason at all, and I was puzzled. It was with a twinge of relief that I finally let my client out of my flat. I had been very honest in some respects and offered some revealing truths for consideration. I felt sure the vicar would not return. I had every intention of making sure we were not in quite such close proximity again. As my pulse rate returned to a reassuring normality, I wondered how on earth my usually stalwart defences had been breached. I had absolutely no idea. The incident was best forgotten. So that's what I attempted. 0 foolish woman!

It was later that summer that my friendly, upstairs neighbour made a remark that made me jump. She was an older lady who had once been married to a Baptist minister. She was as wise and kind as she was educated and humorous. She was also as alert as Lady Bracknell on 'speed'.

"Do you know, I was listening to Andrew preach the other day…at a Women's Fellowship Meeting…" she began, stirring her coffee thoughtfully, "and suddenly, inexplicably, I thought of you. I don't know why." Kind but penetrating blue eyes met mine over the rim of the cup. Somewhere, deep inside, I began lacing up running shoes. Weeks later I was trudging home from work when I passed the Rectory. To my surprise Andrew was working in the front garden. He looked up and smiled as I went past. I had the vivid impression of blue eyes that exactly matched his shirt. To my horror my heart did a backward flip. Squeaking a greeting I stumbled on my way, completely bewildered. What had that been about? It had literally come out of the blue.

Earlier that year, in the small sea side town, another older lady had returned rather thoughtfully to her home after attending a Women's World Day of Prayer service.

I had taken that Service.

"Do you know, dear," she remarked to her husband, hanging up her coat, "I thought what a wonderful wife the lady who took our Service would make for the Vicar".

In the peace and beauty of a retreat centre garden later that year I became gradually aware of the yawning emptiness of my life beneath all my busyness. In that moment the pain of contemplating a life endlessly alone became almost too much to bear. There are people who are called to live alone, and are given the grace to do so; I knew I did not have this grace. I might deny the fact that I had even been given the promise of a husband out of fear but my uncertainty could not negate that promise. Over the intervening years I felt I had been reminded many times, and God never goes back on His Word. I needed to continue waiting and believing.

It was in September that Carol suddenly paused as she was leaving my flat.

"Jenny, may I pray with you a moment?"

I'd long since learnt never to refuse an offer like that, so she prayed and we sat quietly together for a while. When Carol broke the silence, I could tell she was quite serious.

"Jenny, I can see a picture in my mind of a castle. I believe the Holy Spirit is giving me this picture. The castle has a moat round it, and the drawbridge is pulled up". I was suddenly ashamed, and completely convicted. I knew instantly she was describing my attitude of heart. I quietly apologized to God for my fear and unbelief. He had been nudging me a long time about this, but I had been ignoring Him. He could not move without my assent, after all we were co-workers. After I received that forgiveness, it felt as if the drawbridge had been lowered. I had the sense I was standing at an upper room turret window of the castle, Jesus and I were looking out of the window. "Carol," I said awkwardly, "I feel I should be scanning the horizon for a white horse…" She chuckled.

"I don't quite knowhow to say this…but I have another picture now. There's a man with a rowing boat in the castle moat. He's rowing round and round the castle wondering how to gain access". She went on to explain in rather an embarrassed way that she could 'see' a rope from my turret window which led to the boat. I could only nod in astonishment for I could see a rope ladder! Then I realized that my new faithful decision must take me down until I reached the boat…and the man. I was still coming to terms with this truth when I realized Carol had moved from the armchair to the lounge window. She was looking down to the pavement below.

"Look," she said with her gentle smile, "there's Andrew walking his dog."

Chapter 31

Climbing out of the turret window was to prove the most difficult part of my resolution. That winter the flu claimed me with wicked intensity and I had to rely on several close friends at Church for support, provisions and encouragement. This was probably a learning time for me in accepting the care and support of others.

I was particularly friendly with Peter and Paula, a lively couple, who brought me far more than I needed in every sense of the word.

"I met Andrew on my way here," Peter informed me one day as he carried shopping into the kitchen.

"He sends his best wishes. He's such a nice chap, you know."

I stood before, him white and weak in my dressing gown, not appreciating the character reference at all. Peter smiled his warm smile as he put the carrier bag on the table.

He went on cheerfully, "Do you know if someone were to ask me who my best friend was, I think I would say it was Andrew." My non-responsive silence thickened. As soon as he'd gone I paid the loo a greyhound-like visit. I couldn't see what God was up to at all. I couldn't even get to the window, any window, let alone climb out of it. What I hadn't mentioned to my dashing shopper was that days earlier I had received a very amusing "Get Well" card from the Vicar in question.

On the front was a picture of a girl, literally in bed with a bug. It had horns and a ridiculous smile. Deep within, a sort of knowing burst into being, a recognition. "Hope you get rid of it (the bug) soon. Couldn't resist this, love and prayerful good wishes …Andrew. (If there's anything you need or anything I can do, please let me know…)."

I'm nothing if not a fighter. Flu-warped, I decided on one last ditch attempt. I suppose it was a good job God was expecting this approach. I gathered my shaky, recovering frame as Paula drove me back from the next week's supermarket shop.

"Paula, can I be honest with you?" I asked from the passenger seat.

"Of course you can," she said instantly, concentrating on the road ahead.

"Well. I really appreciate you and Peter, all your kindness, but…but I have to say…that there isn't any way that I am going to be linked romantically with Andrew Rose."

I expect a couple of angels collapsed with hysterical laughter. Paula never wavered. She didn't take her eyes off the road.

"Well, my dear, "she said, "God knows." Which, of course, was absolutely right.

As a result of my illness I had learnt afresh about obedience, pride, and dependence on God. Some nights, as I recovered my health, I could not sleep. All I saw was Andrew's face. I told myself that this was all of my humanity, nothing to do with spiritual matters at all. That did not work either.

In case you are jumping up and down, dear reader, in an agony of frustration, I must point out that my greatest fear was a terror of the past repeating itself in a different form. One relationship had disintegrated into unimagined horrors and my mind struggled to believe that another would be different. Andrew came to visit me before I went back to work. I felt a very tiny sense of defeat as I let him out of the flat pointedly thanking him for his 'pastoral' visit. "Don't think of it as that," he said smiling. It was a nice smile. The window ledge looked quite spacious, but that rope had a long drop.

It was just before Christmas that I noticed a huge bunch of flowers and balloons being delivered to the house opposite. I immediately drifted off into a romantic reverie which I have been prone to most of my adult life. How good to have someone care enough to send something like that. A dream, and for most women all it will ever be. A few moments later my front doorbell rang. I took delivery of a huge box. Inside were roses and pine cones in a most beautiful arrangement, accompanied by a card wishing me a "Christ-filled Christmas, from Andrew." The world simply stopped.

"I bet he sends flowers to lots of ladies in the Church," I said weakly to Jen, who had come to stay with me for Christmas. But I didn't fool her, or myself, for a single moment. "But Jenny", she said, "they're roses".

The Strongest Tree

Chapter 32

The tea tray was set and there were mouth-watering biscuits. I had been invited to afternoon tea at the Rectory, and perched awkwardly at one end of the sofa. Andrew at the other end poured some tea and we looked at his new Labrador whom I had come to meet. She sat smiling several feet away from the biscuits. I'd always liked dogs and been interested to hear about the Vicar's new female companion. I'd even bought her a gift-wrapped bone for Christmas. She was, it has to be said, rather beautiful. She had large molten brown eyes, long eyelashes and a soft pale coat. Now she gazed from Andrew to the biscuits, from the biscuits to Andrew, with an expression of worship. "No," he reminded her, "You'll have some supper later." We chatted for a while about dogs, church matters and the excellence of the biscuits. I thought I was doing rather well emotionally as I drained my cup and eventually prepared to leave. Andrew must have sensed the move. He glanced up from his teacup rather shyly.

"Jenny, this might come as a bolt from the blue "(which it didn't)", but I wondered if you would come out for a meal with me one evening?" The edge of the sofa pressed into the back of my legs in the silence. I knew if I didn't say 'yes' immediately I would say 'no'.

"Yes" I said immediately. Andrew beamed. We arranged a time and place. Yet there was something else.

"Um… there is just something I should say…," I said carefully, "I've had a rather difficult past, relationship wise, so I might not find this sort of thing particularly easy …"

"That's all right," said the vicar of the small sea-side town, "perhaps I won't either."

As it happened we both found the dinner date remarkably easy, chatting as the car sped through the darkness to the Pier Hotel in Harwich. I couldn't help composing fantasy newspaper headlines with part of my mind, "Vicar abducts counsellor under cover of darkness," or perhaps, "Secret assignation rocks sleepy town as counsellor's double life is revealed". The whole situation was so unusual. I had not been out on a dinner date for over fifteen years. I couldn't even remember doing so in my twenties either. I had, however, mentioned my daring to one good friend, Mary, who had been praying for me and my future for many years.

"How exciting!" she'd responded, "Need I buy my hat yet?"

We'd always joked about wedding hats.

"Good gracious no, Mary," I said instantly alarmed, "We're just friends. It's good to have friends isn't it?"

A few days later I received a card from her and the text read, "For My thoughts are not your thoughts, neither are your ways my ways, says the Lord (Isaiah 55v8)."

It was both strange and exciting to be eating out with an attractive man. The whole evening seemed from a forgotten world and had a dreamlike quality. I'd got myself a new blouse and skirt from my usual boutique (Oxfam), and I'd brought some new make-up as well. Now I sat before a sparkling white table cloth. There were elegant glasses and the gleam of the cutlery seemed dazzling. I was experiencing the odd feeling of the care and interest of someone who I did not know, but who wanted to know about me. I felt suddenly shy. I would have been shyer if I'd realized that my new make-up had gone all streaky in the combination of wine and excitement.

I learnt later that Andrew had apparently enjoyed the evening and felt that the relationship was "worth pursuing." It was clear that God had been moving in many hidden ways in both our lives before that meal. As I'd walked past the Rectory in the past months Andrew had seen me from the study window. At exactly that time I, all unknowing, had continued to pray for him and his family. Andrew had pondered and prayed. Then he'd warned his supportive family and the Bishop that he intended asking me out. Wanting to be well prepared Andrew had then asked his friends Peter and Paula what they thought my reaction might be at the plan. I can imagine Peter grinning as he replied.

"Well, Paula and I were thinking that this might be what God had in mind as well! Jenny will either say 'yes' or she'll run a mile." It's a little unnerving to be known so well.

The Strongest Tree

Chapter 33

Courting a parishioner in your parish is not without its difficulties. Andrew had warned his surprised Bishop that romance was in the air, and there followed a series of assignations in special places where we got to know more about each other. At first we were both protecting ourselves in case our friendship foundered; the last thing we needed was an eager parish monitoring our every move. However, our meetings developed into a quite thrilling courtship..., 'a little like an affair' one friend sighed afterwards.This struck me as a good description. We were bound by secrecy and excitement, but not in a physical sense.

"Hello Andrew," I'd smile if I met him accidentally in the morning outside his house, "What a lovely day."

"It is, isn't it?".

And to our great delight a parishioner, on the opposite pavement would walk past with her shopping and wave at us. Once, we met outside the supermarket several miles away. "Hello Jenny. Would you like a lift home with that shopping?" "Why, how lovely. Yes please!" We walked, chatting self-consciously to Andrew's car, passing several people we knew. Once inside the car it was hard to stop chuckling.

We both had the same sense of the dramatic and a silly sense of humour.

On Valentine's Day Andrew took me to a splendid meal at a famed restaurant, only to discover half way through the feast that the chef was the son of a church member. Fortunately he stayed in the kitchen!

One afternoon I received a phone call from my observant upstairs' neighbour.

"Er....Jenny. I noticed a huge bunch of flowers outside your door that arrived whilst you were at work the other day…"

"Indeed."

"Am I missing anything…?"

"I don't think so…, a good friend sent them. So kind." I certainly couldn't tell her what she was missing, even when a couple of weeks later she commented about hearing 'a rather masculine voice' below her in my flat.

"Really? Well, I do listen to a lot of teaching tapes you know…it was probably one of those." Whilst I was busy giving an award-winning performance of innocence I'm not sure she was convinced. My jubilant Watford friend suggested she send me some dark glasses and a wig. That was, I understand, when she wasn't break- dancing with joy before the Lord. Personally I was in the grip of mixed feelings.

It was very exciting having a caring man friend, but beneath all the joy and humour of the situation, I had to come to terms with lurking doubts. My doubts had their roots in my previous relationship. How long would care and warmth last?

Did I really want to live life at this pace, or put anyone else (apart from God) before myself? If there was going to be a physical side to the friendship how would I react now? And more mundanely, would my wardrobe or nerve extend to these constant challenges, meetings, meals, drives ..., life now being a whirlwind of ideas, movement and visiting. Days were disappearing in breathless activity and disrupted routine. Previously I seldom left the town. Now I was seldom at home.

I was aware, too, of the danger of neglecting a most important relationship in my life at the expense of this new multicoloured one, that of my relationship with God. Yet I felt encouraged at every point in prayer about my friendship with Andrew and that this was indeed God's plan. This reassured me and smoothed away fears about the future. God was in control and understood me better than I understood myself. He understood Andrew, too.

The time came when Andrew wanted to tell his grown up children, Liz and Tim, about the lady four doors down the road.

"Dad", Tim responded, "you're sounding like a teenager... Go for it! Life is too short." When Andrew told me I thought this a very generous response.

Andrew's daughter, Liz, reacted with characteristic generosity as well.

She was obviously monitoring the new relationship carefully. She texted Andrew one evening to point out that perhaps the film we had chosen to go and see was one for which we were just a little too elderly. She was right. We had great fun, however, deciding which film might suit our more mature tastes or if our Zimmer frames would cope with the journey!

Laughter oiled the wheels of our growing friendship, and when Andrew's 94 year old mother, Millie, was introduced to me on a visit from Yorkshire, I had the strangest sense of falling in love, as her twinkling eyes met mine. Years previously, God had promised me He would make me part of a family again, "by His Spirit." That had seemed humanly impossible. I was too old to have children, after all. But God's ways…. A realm of light, a new truth, was beginning to spread before me as I accepted His way. It involved an open-hearted family and a vicar.

One evening Andrew told me gently that he thought he was falling in love with me. "I…I can't respond in quite the same way yet," I said typically.

I knew I had to be honest, for too much was at stake.

"That's all right. Take your time. I can wait…," he smiled.

Chapter 34

"Jenny," Andrew said one day, "I've some time off soon, and I had planned to drive north for my Godson's wedding, but it's been postponed. I don't suppose you'd like to come with me for the weekend? I know that this is rather short notice…"

"Can I think about it a bit?"

"Of course". There was a great twinkle in his eyes.

I fled back to my flat and phoned the very wise friend, Jessica, who had been with me in the Brighton Community. She, too, had since become a vicar.

"He wants me to go away with him for the weekend!", I squeaked.

"Jolly good."

"WHAT?!"

"Well, what on earth is wrong with that?"

"I don't know… I mean… Is it all right? He's a vicar…," I said lamely. I could feel her amusement pulsing down the line.

"I doubt he'll leap on you with carnal lust, Jenny. A weekend away would do you good, both of you… get to know each other more."

"Oh… I see. You really think so?"

"I really think so. You don't believe I've been pestering God all these years for nothing do you? Go for it. And don't forget to let me know what happens!

The drive to Yorkshire to the family home was memorable because Andrew and I talked and laughed together most of the way. It was as if we were perfectly used to driving hundreds of miles together. I kept sneaking sidelong looks of disbelief at the striking profile of the man beside me. I kept thinking I would wake up any moment. He was interested in me, of all people. I'd heard about Andrew's sister and brother-in-law in their absence but they were unfortunately away from home for

that weekend. They'd thoughtfully arranged for Andrew, Millie and I to be cared for by friends. (Millie lived with them full time.) I instantly warmed towards Andrew's relations without having met them. That has never happened to me before or since, usually I am much more measured in my affections. It was a large house, set in the Yorkshire Pennines. The garden and surrounding hills looked magical at seven o'clock in the morning, bringing 'Lord of the Rings' to mind.

As I drew back the bedroom curtains I felt I had entered a dream. I was in the middle of something I had longed for at least half my life, a romantic adventure one only read about in books. I have to point out that I was up at this time to do my hair before Andrew knocked on the door with a cup of tea. Even a romantic heroine has standards. Actually, I nearly spilled the tea down my dressing gown at the appointed hour because a vicar can look extremely attractive in modern nightwear, especially with tousled hair.

The boundaries of the dream were to be pushed even further later that day.

We decided to visit the Bronte museum at Haworth which was quite near. As we walked across the car park to the small museum Andrew slipped his hand quite naturally into mine. Our togetherness was sealed that evening with a gentle kiss. I could not tell you what we saw that day at the Bronte Museum, but I knew that the floor was made of clouds.

The Strongest Tree

Chapter 35

On the first of April that year I entertained the vicar of the small town for supper.

To my relief, my cooking had met with approval. Then we settled down comfortably to watch a favourite television programme, yet I noted that Andrew seemed rather quiet and pre-occupied. As we looked at the screen my mind began racing.

'I suppose he's wondering how to tell me he's decided our relationship has to finish,' I thought, steeling myself for a crisis.

'Oh well, I'll survive…I have before…'

"Jenny," Andrew said very gently. 'Here we go,' I thought.

"You may want to think about this a while," he went on," but I was wondering how you would feel about marrying me? Just take your time…I needn't know now…".

I didn't need to take more than two seconds. I'd long since realized that I loved him.

"That would be a privilege. Yes, please I'd like to marry you."

He swung me into a great hug and kiss and we both sat staring at each other in shock, like two excited children.

"What shall we do? Who can we tell?"

The next moment we had telephoned Peter and Paula. We ran to the car and were at our friends' house within minutes. There were hugs and tears, whoops and laughter. Peter opened a bottle of Champagne. Andrew was still holding my hand whilst I was in a bit of a daze just sipping the Champagne and smiling. The future had been unleashed and none of us really knew what God would do with what He had planned for so long.

My phone rang at nine o'clock the following morning. It was not my new fiancé.

"Hello Jenny," said Peter carefully, "did you sleep well?"

"I did indeed." Peter knew me very well.

"I was wondering how you were feeling about what happened last night?"

"It's all right Peter...I'm fine. I'm going to marry Andrew. We were wondering if you would give me away?" His relief and joy widened my smile even more.

After we bought the engagement ring Andrew and I agreed on a Sunday to tell the Church. I waited for the final hymn that Sunday feeling tense.

"There is a young lady in the congregation," Andrew announced, then, "who is wearing a new engagement ring." It was, he went on to a fascinated congregation, because she had consented to marry him. There was a profound silence throughout the large building for at least three seconds. Then everyone broke into spontaneous applause. To my horror, Andrew invited me to the front and we stood together.

There were more hugs and astonished cries after the service.

"We never knew you were an item."

"That was the point." Andrew was enjoying himself. I was just as pleased, but felt very vulnerable. For four years I had sat at the back of the Church. Now God had drawn me to the front in an unmistakable way.

"When you tell the eleven o'clock congregation," whispered Carol, sidling up to me in the throng, "Remember, you are allowed to smile!"

The Strongest Tree

Chapter 36

It seemed as if a small violin solo had suddenly joined the orchestra. I had emerged, blinking, into my own fairytale. Now, I constantly met people in the small town who would stand and beam at me, their eyes bright with sentiment and good wishes. "I" had become "us", and delighted parishioners wanted to hear the melody.

Now I accompanied Andrew self-consciously to lunches, meetings, concerts and other social gatherings in a sort of confused trance. I have never been very good with people en mass and now I had lost one of my treasures, privacy. Quite dramatically I had relinquished aloneness, space and the unique privilege of anonymity.

"Who is Jenny?" I heard one elderly lady whisper to her companion at a dinner Andrew and I attended. It was a good question. I hardly knew. Now I was busy designingwedding invitations with Andrew that might honour the God who had brought us together, and checking the eight hundred and forty things that needed to be done for our wedding that October. Yet joy and excitement was lending wings to my life.

One day, Peter and Paula and I went in search of wedding outfits, leaving Andrew firmly at home. I knew the dress I wanted because God had showed me in a dream. As my Matron of Honour, Paula found the most stunning long dress that hugged her enviable figure to perfection. Andrew's daughter, Liz, had kindly agreed to be bridesmaid and in a dress of classic elegance she, too, looked stunning. Where was my outfit? Rather warily, we trooped into one last bridal shop. Hanging opposite the door on a rail was a satin-look mauve jacket and long smooth skirt.

"That's the one!" I cried triumphantly. It was exactly the outfit in the dream.

Any bride-to-be will confirm that wedding preparations are not all plain sailing. Occasionally the sea became decidedly choppy. One day Andrew's sister and several other guests phoned me and reported they had booked into a nearby Hotel. I should have been delighted. The problem was that it happened to be the same Hotel Andrew and I had booked for our Wedding night. I didn't fancy playing 'spot the guest' along the luxurious red plush landings clutching my new floral sponge bag. That same day two guests were unfortunately to be absent through unforeseen circumstances, my wedding dress fitting was cancelled due to lack of staff, and I learnt that the invitations would take a week longer to produce than we had expected. On top of all this Andrew remarked, unwittingly, that I had rather a lot of mauve in my wardrobe.

"…My dress is mauve …"I sobbed down the phone to the ever patient Paula, "He'll hate it…"

"Don't be ridiculous", she said sensibly, "It's lilac anyway. He'll love whatever you wear." It had been a long day.

Andrew and I had a chat with a very talented photographer called Sally. Tall and bubbly, she had taken splendid photos at Tim's Wedding and seemed enchanted by our story. I couldn't fail to be relaxed and confident by her professional approach. She was enthusiastic but very honest.

"The only thing is… I do sometimes cry in Churches," she confided before she left us," "but this is all so lovely…" "I will concentrate extra hard"

God seemed to send folk who had a crackling sense of humour to smooth our way. A lively lady, Penny, had come to cook for Andrew (and iron…) in his time alone at the Rectory. The most enormous, delicious lunches awaited him after a morning's work. He was practical as ever and I would receive a phone call after Penny had gone home for her own meal.

"Luncheon is served". I would walk up to the Rectory and share the Vicar's cordon bleu lunch. We didn't tell Penny until after we were married. She roared with laughter.

"Honestly, why on earth didn't you say…?" "I could have cooked for both of you." I knew if we had, we would have been eating until doomsday.

The Strongest Tree

Chapter 37

"Baths, bedsteads and bishops," Andrew commented as we drove to the bishop's house after some shopping. I had no previous experience of meeting a bishop (I was a Methodist). This rather special bishop and his wife were the couple who had been so supportive of Andrew and his first wife, Pat. There was an air of quietness and warmth about him, gentle humour that put me at ease. His wife, Anne, kindly gave me a beautiful plant, also promising to sit on 'my' side in Church when she learnt I had no family still living. The couple was God's love made visible as we talked together about the service. I was about to be made "family by His Spirit" and God had left no detail unattended in His promise to me.

It was a six months of meetings and departures. Andrew and I visited many of our respective friends together, and they all seemed thrilled at the news of the forthcoming wedding.

"It's repayment time." smiled Mary, reaching for a tissue with a watery smile.

"What do you mean?" I asked.

"Jenny, it's so marvellous of God. Andrew is the healing to so much damage you've suffered over the years. God has met you in every place that was broken." I blinked. I really can be as thick as soup sometimes. As I looked back over my troubled years I began to see that she was right. Perhaps the story had more chapters.

In the middle of meetings and introductions, explanations and rejoicing, there came the time for me to meet Andrew's children. I knew more about them by now and their sensible approach to their Dad's new relationship, but had not actually met them. I wondered if they would be as nervous as I felt.

Andrew and I had just finished a cup of tea at the Rectory one day when Tim and his wife Emma arrived. I remember a great sense of relief as the tall, smiling young man came into the lounge. He was obviously Andrew's son. He had his Dad's easy manner coupled with very perceptive eyes. We soon established that I was a Methodist in a chat about churchmanship.

"You can get ministry for that," Tim said, smiling. I relaxed.

I felt engulfed in a wave of warmth from him and from Emma, whose attractive gentleness soon evaporated any awkwardness. When my own father had mentioned to me his intention of perhaps remarrying several years before his death I had frozen with indignation. Andrew's children obviously came from a different mould. It was near Easter when I was to meet Liz, and I wondered briefly whether I should buy her an Easter egg. Eventually I rejected the idea on the grounds that she might think me too familiar, or that I was treating her like a child. Andrew and I met up with her in the car park of a nearby stately home. We planned to have a relaxing meal together and then wander round the house and gardens. As I got out of the car a young woman in a tailored pink coat came towards me. She had very clear skin and chiselled features. I had the odd, fleeting feeling of facing myself years earlier. Liz was smiling and holding out an Easter Egg.

The Song of Solomon, chapter 2, verses 11-13.

"...for lo the winter is past, the rain is over and gone, the flowers appear on the earth, the time of singing has come, and the voice of the turtledove is heard in our land. The fig tree puts forth its figs and the vines are in blossom, they give forth fragrance. Arise, my love, my fair one, and come away.

Chapter 38

July had been cold, but it was the sunniest October anyone could remember for years. A mist from the sea melted into warm sunshine, and rejoicing slipped into the church garden. No one forgets their wedding day, and I still look back on mine as one of the most special in my life.

"The winter has passed. The spring has come..." God's Word had made it clear to me for years. I was to be a witness to His people of His glory. He was and is a God for whom nothing is impossible.

I don't think I slept the night before, counting the dark hours away at Peter and Paula's immaculate bungalow. Time at the hairdressers fled amid emotional stylists and a special make up session. Sally, the bubbly photographer, sparkled and snapped Liz, Paula, Peter and I in all our finery. Even the fact that two dresses had not, after all, been turned up properly failed to matter. I hitched mine up and did some creative work on Liz's straps with concealed pins. We were far too early getting to the church and the leather in the vintage car that was my transport began to breathe in a deep, intoxicating sort of way. Round the block we went twice, being redirected by Andrew's brother-in-law resplendent in a kilt of imposing proportions. I glimpsed his wife Janet among the parrot-hatted guests looking exactly as if she had just stepped from the fashion pages of 'Vogue'. Today I felt we had both come from the same publication.

Eventually Peter, my gallant 'giver away', stood poised beside me. We all stepped into the Church.

"Jenny", he whispered quietly, "I know I should say something…but I can't think of what to say!" How could I convey that just his reassuring presence was all the steadying I needed. I squeezed his arm. "That's all right, I'm fine."

We walked slowly, almost regally up the long church, and I was calm enough to nod and smile at some familiar hats. I'd chosen 'Jesu, joy of man's desiring'as the music for my entrance because I reasoned that if I put Him first everything else would be fine. It was.

Andrew was waiting and turned and smiled at me, a smile just between us. Mauve did not seem to be a problem after all. We had asked various friends to take part in the service, reading, preaching and singing to glorify God. I kept calm by concentrating very hard. I was not really prepared for the moment I turned round. There seemed to be hundreds of people packing the Church. I saw some smiles, some tears and vividly coloured wedding outfits glowing in the sun that poured through the tall windows.

I was particularly moved that the wedding hat I had joked about for years over the phone with Mary was now a reality. All looked almost unreal. Sally was extraordinary. She was not crying, but my abiding memory of her is of great, unashamed star leaps in the air at the back of the church.

Isaiah 62 Verse 3, 4. "You shall be a crown of beauty in the hand of the Lord, and a royal diadem in the hand of your God. You shall no more be termed Forsaken,

and your land shall no more be termed Desolate, but you shall be called My delight is in her, and your land Married, for the Lord delights in you, and your land shall be married....as the bridegroom rejoices over the bride, so shall your God rejoice over you.

(The prophetic Scripture received five times over fifteen years.)

Quite dazed I turned back to the bishop and the business in hand. He completed the required prayer over Andrew and me as we had knelt before him, and then he despatched the heavy embroidered kneeler to one side with the most accurate football side kick I have ever seen. He had caught the spirit of joy and celebration perfectly in one skilful movement.

The Isaiah prophecy I'd been given five times over the last fifteen years had been fulfilled. Love had drawn me into the heart of a new family. Whilst I'd always yearned for romance I wasn't the sort of woman who read much romantic fiction or sighed over modern love stories. Yet the truth is, if I could have bottled the essence of our honeymoon in Paris, I would have kept the perfume indefinitely.

All the people we met seemed vibrant with life, from the hotel staff to the joyous side-street café proprietor. Our days sparkled with warmth and excitement. Andrew and I toured the city, museums, galleries, the Eiffel Tower, Montmartre, and the British Embassy Church on

Sunday. Or perhaps the life, warmth and excitement was only us, how we were, what we felt, what we experienced together? Paris became, indeed, 'the city of light.'

Every shred of darkness I'd experienced in previous days seemed to melt in a great shining wave of redemption. We both gave God thanks for His blessing. The nights were especially sacred to me. They were miracles of supernatural grace that obliterated past experiences of damage. I was loved after all, desirable, drawn back to the centre of love which gave me confidence and hope for the future.

Chapter 39

I sat at the dining table and wondered what had happened. Life was not all roses. Or perhaps that was part of the difficulty. I was in the middle of somebody else's life, the 'Roses'. I no longer lived in my peaceful flat of course. The Rectory was exactly as my close friend was shown, gabled front, four bedrooms, a study, lounge, and a large shrub-filled garden. There was no doubt I was in the right place. Yet a place totally unfamiliar to me, with a lifestyle that my perfect courtship had completely overlooked. This large house had been somebody else's home, and much of my time was devoured in trying to bring a new sense of home.

I couldn't find space for me in all my new housewifely duties that I wanted to accomplish so perfectly for the man I loved. I, who had rejoiced in being alone(on good days), was no longer alone and always followed from room to room by two large Labradors who craved my attention like lost children. I had none to give, harried by washing, cleaning, and cooking two meals a day. I had only really ever eaten fast food previously, certainly never planned healthy meals.

My lovely husband never ceased to be loving and supportive, but he had his own work to do. I knew I was free to recreate a home, but there never seemed time. When there was, I felt too tired and disorientated to do much creatively … except feel bewildered and not a little resentful. I was like a swan swimming in oil. Feeling lost, I took to heart the address at the wedding which reminded the congregation that God never changes. He is always the same, yesterday, today and forever. That was a rock I could perch on safely as my new life swirled around.

Andrew and I were still in the process of clearing out my flat, as well as two bedrooms in the Rectory now that Liz and Tim had homes of their own. One bedroom inevitably became a junk room. I used to open the door and just stare at the mount of assorted boxes, clothes and furniture. I had always been such a tidy person. I began to feel sad at my inability to sort out clutter and achieve order.

One day, the phone rang whilst I was standing panicking in the bedroom resembling the 'blitz'. It took me some seconds to find the phone buried beneath a pile of discarded jumpers.

"How is it going?" enquired the pleasant voice of the bishop.

"Not terribly good," I gulped candidly.

"The only way is up". His voice was gentle. Yet I felt I was spiralling in the opposite direction.

"What shall I do with all this STUFF, Liz?" I wailed once to Andrews daughter over the phone.

"Just shut the door on it", she said cheerfully. I did just that.

Only Andrew's loving presence and crackling sense of humour salted those days with light. We'd often meet in the kitchen and chorus to each other meaningfully, "Peace! Tranquillity! Creativity!" whilst there never seemed much of any available. Andrew worked hard in the parish and sometimes was obliged to attend different evening meetings as well. It was when he returned that I discovered that television and sport were his potent mood restorers. He needed to relax and recharge, and I wondered why these things had not seemed to feature much in the life of my 'Parisian Prince'. He must have wondered what had happened to the smiling, spiritual lady of four doors down. We began to learn about each other at a new depth, the reality beneath the confetti. As someone once famously said, "there were three of us in this marriage" Andrew, me and God. One of our strengths as a couple is that all three communicate. Kind folk came to help me with household chores. I learnt how to both cook and iron properly due to the humorous patience of Penny. Fay showed me how to clean stairs quickly and effectively, something I have been grateful for ever since. As far as the parish was concerned there were at least three crises, and one devastating death, all as Andrew and I struggled with endless coughs and colds. It was a gloomy winter. Yet most importantly I was in the place that God had prepared with the man He had chosen. And that was enough, just.

Andrew's first wife, Pat, had been greatly loved and respected by the church. I told no one of my troubles, but endeavoured to maintain the image of a vicar's wife that I thought was acceptable. It was some time before I believed Andrew when he said he thought there was no such thing as an 'identikit' vicar's wife. I'd always had an image of such a person. I must do that at least as well as Pat. Thankfully, I gradually realised the futility of such thought processes, and was even able to address a women's meeting, causing them to cry with laughter at my description of the attempts to be the perfect wife. No one is…or the perfect husband.

There came moments of pure encouragement, too.

"Andrew is a changed man" commented an elderly lady after Evensong one Sunday.

"Be encouraged. He was so sad, and now he's different. He's happy.

And his preaching…"

Instead of my usual gentle Christmas shared with Jen, I was now in the eye of a tornado of meetings, services, preparations and expecting four members of my new family for the festivities. Ages ranged from thirty to ninety, not counting two dogs and an understandably rather tired vicar looking forward to his Christmas lunch. "The most favourite meal of the year". All things considered this wasn't the best moment to tell anyone that I'd never cooked a turkey before in my life.

But God knew the situation. Well, He certainly had a grip on the proceedings by the time I'd finished praying, put it that way. I did well on Christmas morning, working on the principle that a turkey is simply an overgrown chicken. I'd cooked dozens of those… Then the potatoes refused to roast, I ran out of gravy granules, and the vegetables went mushy. "All going ok?" Tim had wandered into the furnace-like kitchen, and his casual enquiry was beautifully executed. He was checking out the Christmas lunch. I was, after all, an unknown culinary quantity, and Tim was a very good cook in his own right.

"Absolutely fine", I lied, hauling a frying pan out of a cupboard (I'd have to do the potatoes in that). A few moments later Andrew popped his head round the door. "Everything all right?" he asked cheerily.

"Yes thank you". My smile was a little false now. I was flipping potatoes into oil that was not hot enough, and wondering what was wrong with this new oven (weeks later a design fault was diagnosed). Eventually the new family assembled round the table for the much desired Christmas lunch. I was proud of that table. There was upon it every form of decoration, sauce, serviette, and condiment that would be required and a few things that wouldn't be. I offered up a fervent prayer of thanks. I was trying to forget Andrew's sermon reference to "a new wife, a new cooker" and uncertainty about the quality of his Christmas lunch. "You don't deserve any!" commented a gentleman from the congregation as he left the service. The final straw came when Andrew's mother, Millie, peered over her glasses at my cherished table, then at her own plate. It was steaming with traditional turkey fayre.

"Jenny", she asked with elaborate politeness, "Where is the horseradish sauce…?"

The Strongest Tree

Chapter 40

Whilst I might have been feeling like Bambi, trying to stand upright on a frozen pond in mid-winter, I was actually being very well supported. Friends, family and parishioners were praying. I had the comfort of being in my beloved sea-side town, and my husband was not unaware of the difficulties at all. He had, in fact, been doing some serious thinking and obviously heard the whisper of God in his deliberations.

One day, when I was feeling particularly restless, he dropped into the conversation the possibility of a move, a fresh start somewhere else. To my own amazement I had been wondering the same thing for some time, but not spoken of it.

"Goodness, you considering leaving here", he laughed, "This has to be God…" We thought, talked and prayed, and eventually realised our time in the town might be coming to a close. We would each be leaving a very important part of our lives in the place, but we felt we were being called forward. We prayed with friends, one of them, Carol, through whom God had brought me to the town in the first place.

"Do you know" she said softly, "I don't know where God is taking you both... but I can see in my head a picture of somewhere that has trees meeting over the roads."

We all felt that the God who had cared so carefully for each of us was now saying, "We are starting again."

Andrew searched for the appropriate post; we both went for interviews...and waited. There was a terrific mixture of sadness and hope within us both, not unmixed with gratitude, too, when Christian friends confirmed that we were in line with God's call. We knew God had purposes in bringing us together, for His glory, and wanted to walk in them whatever the human cost. I'd known the tenderness of God's care over many years and marvelled at what He had achieved...there was more to come. He'd never let either of us down. Eventually Andrew and I drove to Devon for an interview. He actually preached a sermon to eight people, at the end of which they made the unanimous decision to offer him the post of part-time team vicar.

It was as we had driven down the Devon country lanes on our way to that interview that we noticed the trees. Tall and thick for miles above the great bends... they met over the road.

Epilogue

This story is focused upon one particular journey of change...mine. I am still reflecting upon its extent and living through all its implications and consequences.

It seems to me that God is a God of change and transformation. He delights in turning darkness to gold. Nothing is too difficult to redeem for those who trust in Him. I am led to acknowledge again the reality of a loving Creator yearning to be involved for good in every life created. I'm sure He values joy and partnership far more than we realise and even gives us the faith to trust in Him.

I have come from being very small (2¼lbs at birth!) and anxious, the victim of mental illness and despair to a place of hope. Once as helpless as the addicts and street folk I lived amongst, I have been re-fashioned as a counsellor. Once I lived in small rooms dark with poverty and the threat of violence, selling my possessions to survive... now a spacious place with needs met afresh. Once I was rejected by others, now embraced more by self, and a new family. One relationship continues to heal the first, one honeymoon cancelled by the glory of the second. It seems no detail is too small. My distress at not having a child is blunted by a recent very new grandchild. The sealed drawbridge of fear has been lowered, and feasts spiritual and literal have become part of my healing experience.

It would be unrealistic to leave out the psychological viewpoint of this journey. I have learned to my cost that a child's own upbringing, surroundings, and emotional development play a huge part in the making of the adult that he or she becomes. The circumstances and difficulty of my birth meant no real bonding for me with my mother, or later with my father, for a variety of unavoidable reasons. Thus I was on a continual search as I grew up for an attachment figure by whom I would never be abandoned! It might be argued that a dependent personality entrenched in addiction, fitted my unconscious agenda to perfection. I hungered for the ultimate relationship. An almost non-existent self worth could be re-established slowly, verified by the meaning that Christianity imparted into my life. I was the child who never felt safe enough to grow up and leave home, and became the home of another child who had never experienced home at all, physically or otherwise. I could prove my worth and value to myself and the world by overcoming an enormous trial, emerging respected and victorious. I would be assured, too, of endless love in the unique relationship I had always sought. Except I wasn't, I didn't, and all didn't work out like that at all. My already shaky scaffolding of immature personality was unbolted carefully and laid pole by pole in the dust. I believe now that we are all in a continuous rebuilding process, and demolition plays an important part. My reasoning rests on a faith in the only secure relationship that exists. Considering the journey from a theological viewpoint, the Master Builder has an intimate knowledge of all His created beings, both at their birth and as He uses them for His purposes. I have come to re-affirm that God always knows what His plans will achieve (my mistakes, too, have been pressed somehow into service for ultimate good).

Over these years my experiences have revealed to me more about the ultimate relationship, the One I sought. The ways of revelation have not always been comfortable, nor comfort available on demand. Yet the certainty is of a reliable loving relationship that encloses all others. By choice I am at last within that desired relationship, travelling as it extends into eternity. The name of the game is restoration through faith, crucifixion is the essential, and the rules were minted when God's Son rose from the grave. God has been raising lives ever since.